The Anglo-Saxon Age: A Very Short Introduction

VERY SHORT INTRODUCTIONS are for anyone wanting a stimulating and accessible way in to a new subject. They are written by experts, and have been published in more than 25 languages worldwide.

The series began in 1995, and now represents a wide variety of topics in history, philosophy, religion, science, and the humanities. Over the next few years it will grow to a library of around 200 volumes – a Very Short Introduction to everything from ancient Egypt and Indian philosophy to conceptual art and cosmology.

Very Short Introductions available now:

ANCIENT PHILOSOPHY Julia Annas
THE ANGLO-SAXON AGE John Blair
ANIMAL RIGHTS David DeGrazia
ARCHAEOLOGY Paul Bahn
ARCHITECTURE Andrew Ballantyne
ARISTOTLE Jonathan Barnes
ART HISTORY Dana Arnold
ART THEORY Cynthia Freeland
THE HISTORY OF ASTRONOMY Michael Hoskin
ATHEISM Julian Baggini
AUGUSTINE Henry Chadwick
BARTHES Jonathan Culler
THE BIBLE John Riches
BRITISH POLITICS Anthony Wright
BUDDHA Michael Carrithers
BUDDHISM Damien Keown
CAPITALISM James Fulcher
THE CELTS Barry Cunliffe
CHOICE THEORY Michael Allingham
CHRISTIAN ART Beth Williamson
CLASSICS Mary Beard and John Henderson
CLAUSEWITZ Michael Howard
THE COLD WAR Robert McMahon
CONTINENTAL PHILOSOPHY Simon Critchley
COSMOLOGY Peter Coles
CRYPTOGRAPHY Fred Piper and Sean Murphy
DADA AND SURREALISM David Hopkins
DARWIN Jonathan Howard
DEMOCRACY Bernard Crick
DESCARTES Tom Sorell
DRUGS Leslie Iversen
THE EARTH Martin Redfern
EGYPTIAN MYTHOLOGY Geraldine Pinch
EIGHTEENTH-CENTURY BRITAIN Paul Langford
THE ELEMENTS Philip Ball
EMOTION Dylan Evans
EMPIRE Stephen Howe
ENGELS Terrell Carver
ETHICS Simon Blackburn
THE EUROPEAN UNION John Pinder
EVOLUTION Brian and Deborah Charlesworth
FASCISM Kevin Passmore
THE FRENCH REVOLUTION William Doyle
FREUD Anthony Storr
GALILEO Stillman Drake
GANDHI Bhikhu Parekh

GLOBALIZATION Manfred Steger
HEGEL Peter Singer
HEIDEGGER Michael Inwood
HINDUISM Kim Knott
HISTORY John H. Arnold
HOBBES Richard Tuck
HUME A. J. Ayer
IDEOLOGY Michael Freeden
INDIAN PHILOSOPHY Sue Hamilton
INTELLIGENCE Ian J. Deary
ISLAM Malise Ruthven
JUDAISM Norman Solomon
JUNG Anthony Stevens
KANT Roger Scruton
KIERKEGAARD Patrick Gardiner
THE KORAN Michael Cook
LINGUISTICS Peter Matthews
LITERARY THEORY Jonathan Culler
LOCKE John Dunn
LOGIC Graham Priest
MACHIAVELLI Quentin Skinner
MARX Peter Singer
MATHEMATICS Timothy Gowers
MEDIEVAL BRITAIN John Gillingham and Ralph A. Griffiths
MODERN IRELAND Senia Pašeta
MOLECULES Philip Ball
MUSIC Nicholas Cook
NIETZSCHE Michael Tanner
NINETEENTH-CENTURY BRITAIN Christopher Harvie and H. C. G. Matthew
NORTHERN IRELAND Marc Mulholland
PAUL E. P. Sanders
PHILOSOPHY Edward Craig
PHILOSOPHY OF SCIENCE Samir Okasha
PLATO Julia Annas
POLITICS Kenneth Minogue
POSTCOLONIALISM Robert Young
POSTMODERNISM Christopher Butler
POSTSTRUCTURALISM Catherine Belsey
PREHISTORY Chris Gosden
PRESOCRATIC PHILOSOPHY Catherine Osborne
PSYCHOLOGY Gillian Butler and Freda McManus
QUANTUM THEORY John Polkinghorne
ROMAN BRITAIN Peter Salway
ROUSSEAU Robert Wokler
RUSSELL A. C. Grayling
RUSSIAN LITERATURE Catriona Kelly
THE RUSSIAN REVOLUTION S. A. Smith
SCHIZOPHRENIA Chris Frith and Eve Johnstone
SCHOPENHAUER Christopher Janaway
SHAKESPEARE Germaine Greer
SOCIAL AND CULTURAL ANTHROPOLOGY John Monaghan and Peter Just
SOCIOLOGY Steve Bruce
SOCRATES C. C. W. Taylor
SPINOZA Roger Scruton
STUART BRITAIN John Morrill
TERRORISM Charles Townshend
THEOLOGY David F. Ford

Available soon:

THE TUDORS John Guy
TWENTIETH-CENTURY BRITAIN Kenneth O. Morgan
WITTGENSTEIN A. C. Grayling
WORLD MUSIC Philip Bohlman
AFRICAN HISTORY John Parker and Richard Rathbone
ANCIENT EGYPT Ian Shaw
THE BRAIN Michael O'Shea
BUDDHIST ETHICS Damien Keown
CHAOS Leonard Smith
CHRISTIANITY Linda Woodhead
CITIZENSHIP Richard Bellamy
CLASSICAL ARCHITECTURE Robert Tavernor
CLONING Arlene Judith Klotzko
CONTEMPORARY ART Julian Stallabrass
THE CRUSADES Christopher Tyerman
DERRIDA Simon Glendinning
DESIGN John Heskett
DINOSAURS David Norman
DREAMING J. Allan Hobson
ECONOMICS Partha Dasgupta
THE END OF THE WORLD Bill McGuire
EXISTENTIALISM Thomas Flynn
THE FIRST WORLD WAR Michael Howard
FREE WILL Thomas Pink
FUNDAMENTALISM Malise Ruthven
HABERMAS Gordon Finlayson
HIEROGLYPHS Penelope Wilson
HIROSHIMA B. R. Tomlinson
HUMAN EVOLUTION Bernard Wood
INTERNATIONAL RELATIONS Paul Wilkinson
JAZZ Brian Morton
MANDELA Tom Lodge
MEDICAL ETHICS Tony Hope
THE MIND Martin Davies
MYTH Robert Segal
NATIONALISM Steven Grosby
PERCEPTION Richard Gregory
PHILOSOPHY OF RELIGION Jack Copeland and Diane Proudfoot
PHOTOGRAPHY Steve Edwards
THE RAJ Denis Judd
THE RENAISSANCE Jerry Brotton
RENAISSANCE ART Geraldine Johnson
SARTRE Christina Howells
THE SPANISH CIVIL WAR Helen Graham
TRAGEDY Adrian Poole
THE TWENTIETH CENTURY Martin Conway

John Blair

THE ANGLO-SAXON AGE

A Very Short Introduction

OXFORD
UNIVERSITY PRESS

Great Clarendon Street, Oxford OX2 6DP

Oxford University Press is a department of the University of Oxford.
It furthers the University's objective of excellence in research, scholarship,
and education by publishing worldwide in

Oxford New York

Auckland Bangkok Buenos Aires Cape Town Chennai
Dar es Salaam Delhi Hong Kong Istanbul Karachi Kolkata
Kuala Lumpur Madrid Melbourne Mexico City Mumbai Nairobi
São Paulo Shanghai Taipei Tokyo Toronto

Published in the United States
by Oxford University Press Inc., New York

Text first published in *The Oxford Illustrated History of Britain* 1984
First published as a Very Short Introduction 2000

British Library Cataloguing in Publication Data
Data available

Library of Congress Cataloging in Publication Data
Data available

ISBN 978-0-19-285403-2

9 10 8

Typeset by RefineCatch Ltd, Bungay, Suffolk
Printed in Italy by
Legoprint S.p.A., Lavis (TN)

Contents

List of Illustrations

The publisher and the author apologize for any errors or omissions in the above list. If contacted they will be pleased to rectify these at the earliest opportunity.

List of Maps

Introduction

Perched on the edge of the fragmenting Roman world, Britain between AD 300 and 700 was at a meeting of currents flowing from several directions. Much of its indigenous Brittonic ('Celtic') population had been under Roman rule, but only in the lowlands of what would be southern and eastern England was it Romanized in any meaningful sense; to the north, Hadrian's Wall was the frontier not merely of Britain but of the Roman Empire. Much of Britain, like Ireland to its west, thus remained a reservoir of Celtic and Pictish culture only superficially touched by Rome.

The attentions of Pictish, Scottish, Frankish, and Scandinavian raiders, barbarians from outside the boundaries of the empire, became increasingly threatening to the authorities in Britain and Gaul during the later fourth century, and would overwhelm them in the fifth. Yet the Roman civilization of Europe was always too close, and too powerful, for even the most primitive invaders to be impervious to it for ever. Sandwiched ambiguously between the pagan barbarian north and the Christian Roman south, the lost province of Britannia became a melting pot of diverse influences. This ambiguity, and this diversity, help to explain the distinctiveness of the early medieval cultures that would take shape in Britain.

Chapter 1
The English Settlements

The sources for the fifth and sixth centuries are few and unsatisfactory in the extreme. On the one hand is the archaeological evidence, mainly objects from graves in pagan cemeteries. This evidence cannot lie, but the questions which it answers are strictly limited. On the other hand is a small group of texts, annals, and fragments. Of these the only substantial contemporary work is *The Ruin of Britain*, a tract written around the 540s by a British monk named Gildas whose purpose was to denounce the evils of his day in the most violent possible language. The Venerable Bede, a monk in the Northumbrian monastery of Jarrow, completed his great *Ecclesiastical History of the English People* in 731. This overshadows all other sources for the seventh and early eighth centuries, and although the invasion period was remote from Bede's own day he provides some surprisingly well-founded scraps of tradition.

The only other narrative sources are fragments of chronicles preserved in later compilations, a few poems, and passing references by Continental writers. The later annals, known collectively as *The Anglo-Saxon Chronicle*, which give a year-by-year summary of events in the southern English kingdoms, contain distant echoes of legend but are highly unreliable before the 570s. Thus the early fortunes of the English can only be glimpsed through the hostile eyes of Britons, through the ill-informed eyes of foreigners, and by means of their own half-remembered traditions. Until the late sixth century, informed guesswork must make do for history.

1. Reconstruction of an early Anglo-Saxon sunken hut at the Weald and Downland Museum, Singleton, Sussex. This was one of the most typical sorts of building in settlements of the fifth to eighth centuries.

Archaeology provides suggestions – still inconclusive and much debated – that Germanic settlers first came to Britain as mercenaries in the late Roman army. The English of later centuries dated their ancestors' arrival some decades after this, and it does seem to have been from the 430s onwards that the immigrants arrived in large numbers. Before considering this remarkable process, it must be asked who the invaders were and what they were like. The first question is answered, almost as well as any modern scholar can answer it, in a startlingly well-informed passage which Bede composed from unknown sources:

> They came from three very powerful Germanic tribes, the Saxons, Angles and Jutes. The people of Kent and the inhabitants of the Isle of Wight are of Jutish origin, and also those opposite the Isle of Wight, that part of the kingdom of Wessex which is still today called the nation of the Jutes. From the Saxon country, that is, the district now known as Old Saxony, came the East Saxons, the South Saxons and the West Saxons. Besides this, from the country of the Angles, that is, the land between the kingdoms of the Jutes and the Saxons, which is called Angulus, came the East Angles, the Middle Angles, the Mercians, and all the Northumbrian race (that is those people who dwell north of the River Humber) as well as the other Anglian tribes. Angulus is said to have remained deserted from that day to this.

In broad terms, archaeology confirms Bede's analysis: objects found in English graves are comparable to those from North Germany and the southern half of the Danish peninsula. Some urns from the fifth-century cremation cemeteries in East Anglia may even be the work of the same potters as urns found in Saxony. A district north-east of Schleswig is called to this day Angeln. To Bede's list we can probably add Frisians, mixed with Saxons who seem to have been infiltrating the coastal settlements of Frisia in the early fifth century. Even Bede's statement that some of the homeland settlements were deserted is confirmed by excavations at Feddersen Wierde, near the mouth of the Weser. Here a village of large timber buildings was abandoned in c.450, apparently in consequence of rising sea-levels. With the natural fertility of lowland Britain, and the evidence that its inhabitants deliberately imported mercenaries, this flooding of coastal settlements suggests a specific context for the migrations to England, though they also have a much broader context in the movements of many barbarian peoples into and across the provinces of the empire.

A Multi-Ethnic Community

Bede's division of the English into ethnically distinct groups is over-neat. The labels which kingdoms and regions later attached to themselves by c.600 – 'Angles', 'Saxons', 'Jutes', and so on – probably indicate the origins of their leaders and elite groups. But archaeology does not suggest that the bulk populations were so clearly differentiated, and by the late sixth century, when the kingdoms emerge into the light of day, there is much blurring at the edges. Thus, the finest metalwork of the East Angles resembles that of Kent, and their royal dynasty seems to have been Swedish. The settlers probably came in small, disparate groups; sea-passage must have weakened ethnic ties, and new types of settlement and social organization developed to suit the needs of pioneer colonists. The precise origins of the settlers mattered less than that they belonged to the same broad culture as southern Scandinavia, Germany, and northern France. Their earliest known poems include hero-legends set in Denmark and Frisia; an early seventh-century East Anglian king possessed Swedish and Gaulish treasures; and the south-eastern English became Christian through a Kentish king's marriage with a Frankish princess.

Here then was a new sort of 'international' community, poised between the Roman and non-Roman worlds. In time the former would reassert its influence, but the earliest Anglo-Saxon generations were essentially a product of the latter. Unlike most of the other 'barbarian' invaders of Europe, the English came from right outside the circle of Roman civilization. The values and social customs which they brought with them would prove astonishingly tough, even through centuries of assimilation to Christian culture. Much that the first-century historian Tacitus wrote of the *Germani* applies to their distant descendants in England. As with the *Germani*, so throughout Anglo-Saxon history, the strongest social bonds were the claims of kinship and the claims of lordship.

Kinship and Lordship

Kin-groups were close-knit in the homeland, and they remained so in England. The families and dependants of one man may sometimes have formed their own settlement units, with shared resources and systems of land-allotment. The influence of such extended 'affinities' on the character of the settlements is shown by the numerous place-names ending *-ing*, *-ingham*, and *-ington*. Hastings means 'the people of Haesta', Reading 'the people of Reada', Wokingham 'the farm of Wocca's people', and so on. Although it is unlikely that these names belong to the first settlement phase, many are early and important and refer to large tracts of land. They show that when territories came to be defined, it was often in terms of the tribal groups which had settled them. Society developed, but family loyalties remained vital. Safety lay in knowing that relatives would avenge one's death, and to neglect such vengeance meant undying shame. Already in Tacitus's day, however, honour might be satisfied by a payment by the slayer to his victim's kin, the *wergild* of later Anglo-Saxon law and custom.

Tacitus also stresses the loyalty of the *Germani* to their lords. Sometimes they had hereditary kings, but in battle they were usually led by elected chiefs: 'It is a lifelong infamy and reproach to survive the chief and withdraw from the battle. To defend him, to protect him . . . is the essence of their sworn allegiance.' Nine centuries later, in 991, an Anglo-Saxon army was defeated by Vikings at Maldon on the Essex coast. By then England was a civilized state, long since Christianized; yet the words which a contemporary poet ascribes to one of the defenders after his leader's death are a clear echo of Tacitus:

> I swear that from this spot not one foot's space
> Of ground shall I give up. I shall go onwards,
> In the fight avenge my friend and lord.
> My deeds shall give no warrant for words of blame
> To steadfast men on Stour, now he is stretched lifeless,
> – That I left the battlefield a lordless man,
> Turned from home. The irons shall take me,
> Point or edge.

Clearly, loyalty to lord might sometimes conflict with loyalty to kin. In the interests of good order and their own authority, later kings tended to promote lordship: thus King Alfred's laws allow any man to 'fight on behalf of his born kinsman, if he is being wrongfully attacked, except against his lord, for that we do not allow'. But on both counts, Anglo-Saxon society always set great store by faithfulness and the keeping of oaths.

Religion

The principal gods of Anglo-Saxon society were those of later Norse mythology, Tiw, Woden, and Thor. They are remembered in the day-names Tuesday, Wednesday, and Thursday, as well as in a few place-names (Tuesley (Surrey), Wednesbury (Staffs), Thursley (Surrey), etc.) which presumably indicate cult centres. Even when converted, the English named one of the main Church festivals after their old goddess Eostre. Shrines, like those of the *Germani*, were in remote places, in woods or on hills: a few place-names include the element *hearg* (shrine), as at Peper Harow (Surrey) and Harrow-on-the-Hill. Since later Church councils forbade the veneration of 'stones, wood, trees and wells', it can be presumed that such activities featured in pagan English cults. At least in its outward forms, this religion does not look so very different from that of the pagan Britons under Roman rule.

Before *c*.600

The narrative of events before *c*.600 does not amount to much. Plagued by the Picts and Scots, says Gildas, the British under the 'proud tyrant', Vortigern, imported the first Saxons to defend the east coast. Bede and other sources add that the Saxons were led by brothers named Hengest and Horsa, who founded the kingdom of Kent, and date their landing to about 450. Although this is rather too late, the tale is very consistent with the archaeological evidence: if Germanic mercenaries were settled under Roman rule, it is entirely likely that the successor states continued the same policy. Then, according to Gildas, the mercenaries rebelled and attacked their hosts; many years of inconclusive warfare followed, culminating in a major British victory, perhaps in *c*.500, at an unidentified place called *Mons Badonicus*. Thereafter, says Gildas, there was peace until his own time, 50 years later, when there were five British kingdoms ruled by wicked 'tyrants'. How far their power still extended into the future English lands is debated, but the refortification of hilltop sites in the south-west points to a warrior society which had reverted to something very like its character in the pre-Roman Iron Age.

One figure from these years who is familiar to everyone is, of course, Arthur. Unfortunately he has only the most shadowy claims to historical reality. The two or three possible fragments of genuine tradition were written down centuries later, and the legends which have gathered around his name are romantic inventions. We can only say that there seem to have been memories of a British war-leader called Arthur, who was associated with the battle of *Mons Badonicus* and subsequent campaigns. Possibly there was such a chieftain or over-king, the last man to unite the former Roman province before it collapsed finally into a patchwork of British and Anglo-Saxon states. So general is our ignorance of major political events that there seems little point in speculating further.

From the English perspective, the *Chronicle* notes the arrival of other chieftains on the south coast, the semi-legendary ancestors of later kings: Aelle in Sussex in 477, and Cerdic and Cynric in Wessex in 495. The next few generations saw a slow but steady advance into the interior of southern and eastern Britain which can be traced, in so far as it can be traced at all, through excavated cemeteries: up the Thames valley, westwards from East Anglia, northwards from the south coast. In the upper Thames valley, disparate English groups were coalescing by the 570s into a federation known as the *Gewisse*, whose advances against the British into Wiltshire and Gloucestershire are remembered in the late annals of the *Chronicle*. Meanwhile, other English kingdoms were emerging from the shadows: the East Angles, the East Saxons, the Mercians, and the Northumbrian kingdoms of Bernicia and Deira. By

2. Monument at Castelldwyran, south-west Wales. The inscription, 'the memorial of Vortipor the Protector', commemorates the 'tyrant of the Demetae' attacked by Gildas.

around 600 we are again on the firm ground of some reliable facts, and find the invaders in permanent control of half the island.

British Survival

What had happened to the native peoples? Sixth-century Scotland was still mainly Pictish, though the settlements of Irish (the future 'Scots') on the west coast had created a settled kingdom, Dalriada. Centuries later, a king of Dalriada was to initiate the formation of a united Scotland. There were also three northern British kingdoms: Strathclyde, centred on Dumbarton, Rheged on the Solway Firth, and Elmet in the region of Leeds. Northumbrian designs on the Picts were ended by a major defeat in 685, and expansion here was mainly at the expense of the Britons. Strathclyde survived, but Rheged and Elmet were swallowed up by Northumbria during the late sixth and seventh centuries.

The main British enclave was, of course, Wales. Refugees from the east had doubtless swelled its population. Christianity survived, and with it some distinct traces of Roman culture. Scores if not hundreds of little monasteries were probably founded there during the sixth century, and charters from south-east Wales suggest the continuance of functioning Roman estate units. The kingdoms of Gwynedd, Dyfed, Powys, and Gwent existed by c.550, and some minor kingdoms by the end of the century. At least two of Gildas's tyrants ruled in Wales: Maglocunus (Maelgwn) of Gwynedd, 'first in evil, mightier than many both in power and malice', and Vortipor (Gwrthefyr) of Dyfed. Vortipor's monument still remains in a Dyfed churchyard – a reassurance that some substance underlies the rantings of Gildas:

> Your head is already whitening, as you sit upon a throne that is full of guiles and stained from top to bottom with diverse murders and adulteries, bad son of a good king . . . Vortipor, tyrant of the Demetae. The end of your life is gradually drawing near; why can you not be

> satisfied by such violent surges of sin, which you suck down like vintage wine – or rather allow yourself to be engulfed by them? Why, to crown your crimes, do you weigh down your wretched soul with a burden you cannot shrug off, the rape of a shameless daughter after the removal and honourable death of your own wife?

Cornwall, Devon, and Somerset formed the British kingdom of Dumnonia. Its king, according to Gildas, was as bad as the others: 'Constantine, tyrant whelp of the filthy lioness of Dumnonia'. The inhabitants were pushed back by the Anglo-Saxons during the seventh and eighth centuries, though Cornwall held out until the 810s. Thanks to this relatively late conquest, something of British culture survived. Excavation suggests that in and around some of the old cities, especially Exeter, Dorchester (Dorset), and Ilchester, life of a sort trickled on through the fifth and sixth centuries. Many major churches in these counties have Celtic origins: excavations at Wells in 1978–80 revealed a sequence of religious buildings from a late Roman mausoleum to the Anglo-Saxon cathedral. Here, as in Wales, smaller churches can often be traced back to a Celtic monastic enclosure (*llan*) or a cemetery around a martyr's grave (*merthyr*).

The hardest task is to estimate British survival in the regions which were firmly Anglo-Saxon by 600. From the facts that England in 1086 probably contained less than half its late Roman population, and that even this was after growth during the tenth and eleventh centuries, it is difficult to avoid concluding that depopulation in the fifth and sixth centuries was indeed drastic. Many fled westwards, or else to Brittany, and epidemic disease may have played its part. More generally, the Romano-Britons simply suffered a common fate of shattered societies; the decline in numbers is perhaps the clearest sign that their society *was* shattered. This is not to say that none remained: there are hints that the population contained substantial British elements, especially in the north and west. Sometimes (in the early Kentish laws, for instance) they appear as peasants or perhaps semi-servile labourers. Significantly, the

English word *wealh* ('Welshman', i.e. Briton) came to mean 'slave', making it hard to know whether the place-name Walton means 'the Britons' settlement' or 'the slaves' settlement'. However numerous, they were subservient: little of their culture passed to the Anglo-Saxons, and almost none of their language.

The Fading of Roman Britain

The early Anglo-Saxons were a non-urban people: their important places were important for hierarchical rather than economic reasons. But the view that they looked on the crumbling Roman towns with nothing but superstitious fear goes too far. The English knew what a *ceaster* was (the word is used with remarkable consistency), and often they knew its Roman name: *Mamucion* becomes *Mame-ceaster* (Manchester), *Venta* becomes *Ventan-ceaster* (Winchester), and so on. Towns occupied focal points in the road system and their walls were strong: they were good places for war-leaders to defend. Yet it is impossible to make a case for the survival of anything that can sensibly be called 'urban life', and tracing any kind of continuous occupation inside Romano-British towns is extraordinarily difficult. (A possible exception is Canterbury, but in this respect as in others its post-Roman development was more like that of a Gallic than a British city.) Eventually some of them would be used as sites for cathedrals and monasteries, but this seems to be more a matter of readoption than of any genuine continuity.

Why was Roman Britain obliterated so much more completely than Roman Gaul? One reason is that the settlers were different: the Franks and Visigoths had come to know far more about Roman ways than the Angles and Saxons ever did. But it is also likely that the Britons themselves had changed greatly between the early fifth and mid-sixth centuries. Only lowland Britain had ever been truly Romanized, and the leaders of the successor states after 400 seem mainly to have come from remoter and more primitive zones. The earliest Welsh poems show a society remarkably like that of the Anglo-Saxons, dominated by the same loyalties and with the same emphasis on treasure, gift-giving, and the fellowship of warriors in their chieftain's hall. Even if no Saxon or Angle had ever set foot in Britain, it is likely that its Roman civilization would have proved too fragile to last.

Chapter 2
The Seventh Century

The years around 600 saw rapid changes in material culture. Kings started building great timber halls, and being buried in barrows with rich treasure; the art of the English was opened to new influences from Europe, Ireland, and even the British. Political, economic, and cultural change should be seen as part of a package, of which the last major element would be put in place when the rulers of the English accepted Christianity.

Kings and Kingdoms

The first impression of early seventh-century England is that it was divided into large kingdoms: Kent, Sussex (the South Saxons), Wessex (the West Saxons), East Anglia, Essex (the East Saxons), Mercia (including the Middle Angles), and Northumbria (comprising Bernicia and Deira and, a little later, Lindsey). Reality was not quite so neat. Kingdoms were only gradually emerging from a state of flux: Middlesex, for instance, is probably the remains of a much larger Mid-Saxon territory dismembered before any surviving records could note it. There were also an unknown number of smaller peoples, lying between the big kingdoms or absorbed within them. Some, like the Hwicce of Worcestershire and the Magonsaete of the Welsh border, had their own kings who were gradually subordinated as the 'sub-kings' or 'aldermen' of greater rulers. There may have been many others: Surrey, for

Map 1. England in c.600.

instance, makes a single appearance as a sub-kingdom in the 670s. Sometimes we can see the continuing self-identity of provincial groups, and their resentment against the bigger powers. Bede says that in 643 a monastery in Lindsey refused to receive the Northumbrian King Oswald's corpse, since although they knew he was a holy man 'he had come from another province and had taken authority over them'. It is possible that in 600 English kings could be counted in dozens.

Even the big states experienced a shifting power balance. Bede and other sources mention a series of over-kings, originating from various kingdoms but successively wielding some sort of lordship over all or most of the Anglo-Saxon peoples. This kind of dominance could be very extensive, but was characteristically short-term. The first four in Bede's list, Aelle of Sussex, Ceawlin of the *Gewisse*, Æthelberht of Kent, and Raedwald of East Anglia, bring us to the 620s. We cannot say what their authority may have meant outside their own kingdoms, though we know that in 616 Raedwald took an army through Mercia, and defeated the Northumbrians on their own frontier. The fifth and sixth were both Northumbrian rulers, Eadwine (616–32) and Oswald (633–42). These are Bede's heroes, his models of victorious Christian kingship. It is with them that we first get a clear idea of relations between the English kingdoms.

Northumbrian expansion westwards led Mercia to make common cause with the Welsh. In 632 Cadwallon, Christian British king of Gwynedd, and Penda, pagan Anglo-Saxon king of Mercia, won a short-lived victory over Northumbria, but the following year Oswald recovered power and Cadwallon was killed. The Welsh continued to support Penda, and in 642 Oswald was slain campaigning far from home. This fact, and an incidental reference to his relations with the king of Wessex, show that Oswald's lordship and military activities extended far outside Northumbria. A group of early Welsh poems give the other side of the story from Bede's: his heroes are their aggressors. In the lament for Cynddylan, a nobleman from Powys who seems to have died in Penda's service, we glimpse the Northumbrians through British eyes:

> My brothers were slain at one stroke,
> Cynan, Cynddylan, Cynwraith,
> Defending Tren, ravaged town
> . . .
> More common was blood on the field's face
> Than ploughing of fallow
> . . .
> The hall of Cynddylan, dark is the roof,
> Since the Saxon cut down
> Powys's Cynddylan and Elfan . . .

In 655, Penda was defeated and killed by the Northumbrian Osuiu, Bede's seventh over-king, who thereafter enjoyed great influence over the other kingdoms. Nonetheless, the rising star was Mercia. The Mercian nobility soon expelled Osuiu and chose Penda's son Wulfhere as their king. By the early 670s Wulfhere seems to have dominated the southern English kingdoms, and in 679 his successor won a victory at the Trent which finally ended Northumbrian expansionism. In the south, however, Mercian power was abruptly checked by the emergent Wessex, which came into existence through a coalescence of Hampshire and Wiltshire Saxons with the *Gewisse* of the upper Thames. Mercian pressure from the north seems to have stimulated a regrouping of these people around a new heartland in the region of Winchester and Southampton Water. The new stature of the West Saxons is evident in the short reign of Caedwalla (685–8), who annexed Kent, Surrey, and Sussex, and in that of his successor Ine. The solid power-base which they built in the south was to determine the fate of England two centuries later.

Aristocratic Life

In the world of seventh-century politics, then, it was possible to gain great power but hard to keep it for long. Why did kings rise and fall so quickly? One reason is that power and conquest depended on military forces; forces were attracted by gift-giving; gift-giving depended on wealth; and wealth in its turn was gained by power and conquest. Society was riddled with feuds, and the succession to kingdoms was fluid and uncertain; hence there were many royal and noble exiles from their own kin in search of generous and congenial lords. King Oswine of Deira, says Bede, 'was tall and handsome, pleasant of speech, courteous in manner, and bountiful to nobles and commons alike; so it came about that . . . noblemen from almost every kingdom flocked to serve him as retainers'. Such a system could hardly be stable: when a king grew sick, poor, or mean his retinue would collapse, and his heirs,

3. Detail of the Sutton Hoo whetstone. This unique object may have been used as a sceptre, possibly modelled on Roman staves of office.

if they survived at all, would become sub-kings or followers of a new lord.

What kingly magnificence could mean is brought to life by the great barrow-burial at Sutton Hoo on the East Anglian coast. It seems to date from around the 620s, and is on the whole most likely (though this is perennially controversial) to have been the tomb of King Raedwald, the fourth in Bede's list of over-kings. He was buried in a ship under a great mound, with his armour, weapons, and a mass of incomparable treasures. The gold and jewelled ornaments are the finest of their kind surviving in northern Europe, and no less remarkable is the range of countries from which items in the barrow came. Sutton Hoo shows that poetic accounts of royal wealth contain no exaggeration. Nonetheless, it should not be seen as a traditional and retrospective monument. Such princely barrow-burials were a new phenomenon around 600, the mark of growing social hierarchy and developing political power; many of the Sutton Hoo objects refer not to the barbaric past, but to the Roman civilization of Christian Europe in which Anglo-Saxon elites were becoming rapidly more interested.

From its beginnings, English society included a military aristocracy, probably with some kind of territorial base. But in the early centuries the king's followers or 'thegns' were tied less to their estates than to the king himself. They were expected to accompany him, to witness his public actions, to live in his hall, and if necessary to fight and die for him. Aristocratic life was strongly communal: the great hall as a place of good cheer, a haven in a dangerous world, is a powerful image in Anglo-Saxon writing. Nobody puts it better than Bede, in the famous words which he gives to a Northumbrian nobleman who is urging King Eadwine to accept Christianity:

> This is how the present life of man on earth, King, appears to me in comparison with that time which is unknown to us. You are sitting feasting with your ealdormen and thegns in winter time; the fire is

burning on the hearth in the middle of the hall and all inside is warm, while outside the wintry storms of rain and snow are raging; and a sparrow flies swiftly through the hall. It enters in at one door and quickly flies out through the other. For the few moments it is inside, the storm and wintry tempest cannot touch it, but after the briefest moment of calm, it flits from your sight, out of the wintry storm and into it again. So this life of man appears but for a moment; what follows or indeed what went before, we know not at all.

The company in the royal or noble hall provided the audience for a literature which mirrored the age: heroic lays recited by professional bards. The surviving fragments include one major epic, *Beowulf*. As we have it, this is a relatively late and sophisticated work, perhaps written for a clerical audience. Yet it lays before us the heroic, essentially pagan world of the seventh-century aristocracy, transmuted by Christianity but not effaced. Its hero, Beowulf, comes to the court of Hrothgar, king of the Danes, to rid him of a monster. A generous giver of treasure and splendid weapons, Hrothgar attracts to his court noble warriors who make him powerful. But the political world of the poem is violent and unstable: a king who loses support will quickly perish, and his kingdom with him. The ethos is one of loyalty and feud: 'It is better for everyone that he avenge his friend, rather than mourn him long . . . let he who can win glory before death.' Beowulf fights with monsters and dragons, inhabitants of a pre-Christian mental world. When he is killed, his followers lay him with rich treasures in a mound overlooking the sea, just as the East Angles had done for their king on the headland at Sutton Hoo:

Then the warriors rode around the barrow
. . .
They praised his manhood and the prowess of his hands,
They raised his name; it is right a man
Should be lavish in honouring his lord and friend.
. . .

They said that he was of all the world's kings
The gentlest of men, and the most gracious,
The kindest to his people, the keenest for fame.

Local Government and Society

But there was more to early Anglo-Saxon society than warfare, savage loyalties, and ostentatious splendour. In some ways this was a surprisingly orderly world. The institutions which made the English State so exceptionally strong in the central Middle Ages have roots in the seventh century or even earlier: the efficiency of 'local government' was one important reason why new overlords could establish power so quickly. The kingdoms seem to have been subdivided into coherent administrative districts, great blocks of 50 to 100 square miles, which apparently existed by the mid-seventh century and may often have originated as the territories of kin-groups. These have long been recognized in Kent, but recent research has detected them also in Northumbria, Mercia, Wessex, Sussex, and Surrey. To a central settlement, with buildings to accommodate the itinerant court, the inhabitants of each district would have looked for justice, and there they would have paid their dues and other public burdens in accordance with a complex system of assessment. Land was reckoned in 'hides', each notionally the area needed to support a free peasant cultivator and his family, and often an actual farm unit. Obligations were assessed by the hide, and hides were grouped into multiples of ten or more which owed obligations of a specialized kind. The king's deputy at the centre might thus receive renders of grain from some groups of hides, of calves or foals from others, and of honey, mead, or lesser commodities from others again. Whatever the origins of this startlingly comprehensive system for dividing up the countryside – which are still much debated – it remains an oddly stable substratum in an unstable political world.

Thus the early administrative districts were organized for exploitation as well as for jurisdiction. A system of economically specialized zones suited the under-developed countryside, with its sharp geographical contrasts and large areas of uncleared common pasture. So it is not surprising that when mid-Saxon kings granted away blocks of land, these early 'manors' often preserved the internal structure of the districts from which they were formed. Hence the 'multiple estate', the federation of distinct 'vills' or townships linked to one manorial centre, which was still prominent in many parts of England in the twelfth and thirteenth centuries. This type of estate structure bears a strong resemblance to that of medieval Wales, and at a basic level some continuity from Romano-British rural organization is quite possible. It is probably misleading, though, to define it too much in ethnic terms. Such 'extensive lordship' was appropriate to under-exploited landscapes with broadly defined economic zones, whether in British or in English areas. It was growth and social change, not Anglicization, which eventually made the 'multiple estate' obsolete.

This pattern also suited a peasant population which was dispersed, unstructured, and relatively small. The most prominent figure in the early sources is the free peasant farmer or *ceorl* (modern English 'churl', but without its derogatory sense), typically cultivating one hide of land. This does not mean that all seventh- and eighth-century farmers were so 'free' that they had no lord save the king. After the Conversion kings granted blocks of land to churches, as they had probably done to lay followers (at least on a temporary basis) from earlier still, and such proprietors must have been concerned to exploit the land thus acquired for their household and other needs. But in these first stages of 'manorialization' it seems likely that lesser lords and churches, like kings, drew revenue from smallholders without greatly altering their way of life or farming methods. There is no evidence for organized 'village communities', nor for the hierarchical, thoroughly dependent groups of tenants who existed by the tenth century. Archaeology suggests that most farmsteads in mid-Saxon England were either isolated or in little clusters, and even the nucleated settlements lack any sign of the orderly streets, greens, and plot-boundaries familiar from later village topography. It now seems likely that medieval common-field systems, with holdings intermixed in scattered strips, result from several centuries of evolution. In seventh-century England the integrated 'village community' was still far in the future.

Chapter 3
Christianity and the Monastic Culture

During three or four generations starting in the 590s, all the English kings and their courts converted to Christianity. Bede's narrative of this process is simple and inspiring: Italian and Frankish missions in the south; Irish missions in the north; triumphant unity after the settling of liturgical disputes in 664. The reality was more complicated, and more conditioned by political and cultural factors, than Bede allows. In the complex melting pot that was Britain, Christian influences are likely to have reached the English from a variety of sources at once – even from the despised British, whom Bede systematically excludes from his story. Economic and political contacts led; the Cross followed: Kent was already exposed to the Christian culture of Frankish Gaul, Northumbria to that of Scottish Dalriada. More generally, the English, with their recently developed kingdom structures and social hierarchies, were now ripe for conversion to a hierarchical, top-downwards religion which would make them eligible to join the club of civilized Christian peoples.

Conversions

The mission which a Roman monk named Augustine led to Kent in 597 was launched by the expansionist papacy of Gregory the Great, who according to tradition had seen English youths in Rome and pronounced them 'not Angles but angels'. This was no voyage into the unknown. King Æthelberht already had a Christian Frankish queen; his baptism followed speedily, and Augustine founded a monastery at Canterbury. Misjudging the survival of Romano-British life, Gregory had planned archbishoprics based on London and York, but political realities were acknowledged in 601 when Augustine was enthroned as first archbishop of Canterbury. Initially, success seemed rapid. In 604 a see was founded at Rochester; the East Saxons were converted, and a cathedral dedicated to St Paul was built for them in London. Meanwhile several monasteries were built in Kent, their churches closely modelled on Roman prototypes.

But the Church experienced losses as well as gains. The East Saxons soon apostatized and expelled their bishop. King Raedwald of the East Angles was baptized, but seems to have incorporated Christ into his existing pantheon: Bede reports that he maintained simultaneously a Christian altar and a pagan shrine. In Northumbria the story is similar. King Eadwine received the Roman missionary Paulinus, and was baptized with his thegns in 627. But on his defeat and death only five years later, his successors apostatized and Paulinus had to flee. The Church had speedily gained a foothold in the English courts; but a broader basis was needed if it was to rise above the ebb and flow of political fortunes.

It was Irish ecclesiastics, especially from Scottish Dalriada, who decisively converted the northern English, and who were probably most successful in establishing grass-roots religious contact with the English generally. Since the fifth century Irish Christianity had flourished, especially in the formation of locally based monastic structures. By 600 the Irish monasteries had reached a level of wealth and sophistication far surpassing their counterparts in Wales, and had already established offshoots in Italy, Gaul, and Scotland. For the Christian future of Britain the decisive mission was that of Columba, who went to Scotland, converted the northern Picts (the southern Picts were already Christian), and in *c*.563 founded a monastery on the island of Iona. When the Christian King Oswald won control of Northumbria in 633 it was naturally to Iona that he turned for a missionary, for his exile had been spent among the Irish of western Scotland. It was thus that the Irish monk–bishop Aidan established an episcopal seat on the island of Lindisfarne.

Bede's portrait of the simple, holy Irish ecclesiastics, and their success in communicating spiritual values to the uneducated English, has conditioned historians' thinking ever since. But there is a wider context which helps us make sense of their achievement. Unlike missionaries from Italy and Gaul they came from a tribal, warrior society not unlike that of the English, non-urban and economically undeveloped. It is hardly surprising that they slotted more readily into the aristocratic culture of their hosts than clerics whose background was in Mediterranean cities. Likewise, the monastery as the fundamental unit of religous organization and settlement made more sense to the kin-based English than did the Roman model of a bishop running his diocese bureaucratically from an urban cathedral: after all, an abbot was the father of his family like any Germanic lord. In all the English kingdoms, however converted, the monastic culture would flourish spectacularly during the next century; but effective dioceses would be hard to achieve.

Under the guidance of Aidan and his successors a network of monasteries was established through Northumbria, and the over-kingships of Oswald and of Osuiu enabled this tradition of Christian life to spread into other kingdoms. In the 630s Oswald's influence caused Cynegils of Wessex to accept baptism from an Italian missionary, Birinus, who became first bishop of the West Saxons. Thanks to Osuiu, the East Saxons reconverted and received a Northumbrian bishop named Cedd, who had been trained in the Irish Church. Penda of Mercia remained pagan but allowed a mission from Lindisfarne to work in his realm, and his son Peada was baptized in 653. By 660 only the men of Sussex and the Isle of Wight remained pagan, and soon they too were converted.

Church Organization

As the spheres of Irish and Roman influence spread, tension was probably inevitable, but the main sticking point was an issue which now seems absurdly trivial: on which date should Easter be celebrated? The Irish and British had adopted computations different from those used at Rome, with potentially inconvenient results: at the Northumbrian court the Irish-trained King Osuiu sometimes celebrated Easter while his Kentish-trained wife was still observing Lent. At the Synod of Whitby (664), Osuiu of Northumbria came down in favour of the Roman party, and adherents of the Irish Easter were henceforth increasingly marginalized. If Whitby was possibly not quite such a watershed as Bede would have us believe, liturgical uniformity was certainly an important step in the English Church's coming of age as a united and uniting force through the various kingdoms.

Nonetheless, the Church was beset with problems in the 660s. Organization was haphazard; there were far too few bishops, and some were invalidly consecrated. Others died in a plague in 664, which also made the East Saxons apostatize again. But in 669 the pope sent a new archbishop, a distinguished scholar from Asia Minor named Theodore. During his 30-year reign, this surprising candidate rationalized the diocesan structure, which had been fluid everywhere and perhaps almost absent from kingdoms converted by the monastically organized Irish. Bishops with invalid orders were disciplined, and dubious authorities either ratified or annulled: all acts of the Welsh bishops, for instance, were declared void. A synod held at Hertford in 672 established the first basic canons for Church government. For a brief but brilliant generation, a cathedral school in Canterbury taught the learning of the Mediterranean world.

Theodore had an uphill struggle against vested interests, especially those of the formidable Wilfrid, bishop of the new see of York. Wilfrid was firmly orthodox and had championed the Roman Easter at Whitby, but he resented any threat to his power in the Northumbrian Church. His stormy relations with Theodore and successive kings involved two expulsions, two appeals to Rome, exile, and imprisonment. Meanwhile he managed to preach to the Frisians, convert Sussex, and found a network of monasteries extending through several kingdoms. With his retinue and huge wealth, Wilfrid seems an extraordinary mixture of saint and secular nobleman. Only a young and essentially aristocratic Church could have produced such a figure.

The Monasteries

The 660s initiated a golden age for English monasteries. On the one hand, the Irish-founded houses such as Lindisfarne and Whitby were increasingly influenced by Roman ways, though the old values lived on: in St Cuthbert the solitude and austere devotion of the Irish missionaries was combined with Roman attitudes to monastic life and discipline. On the other hand, many new houses founded in these years would be counted for centuries among the greatest in Britain. Pre-eminent were Monkwearmouth and Jarrow, founded by Benedict Biscop, a Northumbrian nobleman turned monk. Biscop had been five times to Rome, and his twin monasteries brought to Northumbria the culture of the Mediterranean Church. Their most celebrated member, Bede himself, describes how Biscop had a church built by Gaulish masons 'in the Roman manner which he always loved', filled it with rich pictures and furnishings, and built up a great library from Continental sources.

Impressive though these achievements were, there was also a need to provide some permanent basis for the Church's work in the countryside. Here too, the first stages were achieved by monastic or quasi-monastic bodies. Today it seems obvious that missionary work and pastoral care are activities for priests, not monks. But in the seventh and eighth centuries religious communities, often diverse bodies comprising priests as well as monks and nuns, emerged as the natural units of ecclesiastical organization of all kinds. Through the Christian

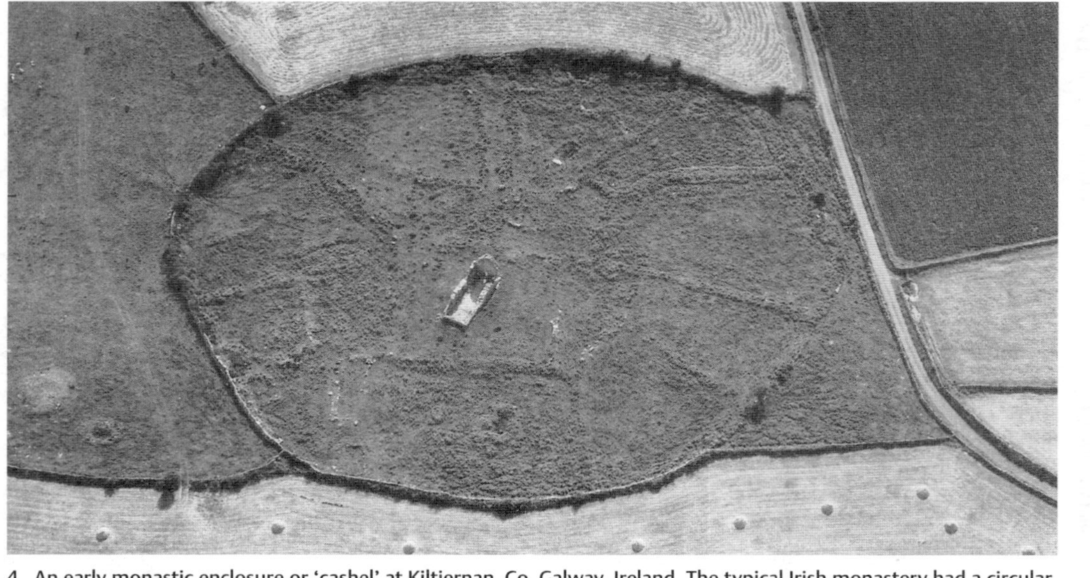

4. An early monastic enclosure or 'cashel' at Kiltiernan, Co. Galway, Ireland. The typical Irish monastery had a circular outer boundary, with an inner precinct for the main buildings. Round monastic sites also existed in Wales and Cornwall, where they are often identified by the place-name element *llan*.

Anglo-Saxon period the word 'monastery' (Latin *monasterium*, English *mynster*) covered institutions ranging from true Benedictine houses to small, loose-knit communities of priests. Rules varied greatly (Biscop composed his own for Jarrow), and so did standards; we really have very little idea of what life was like in all but the greatest houses. But there are good grounds for thinking that by 750 England contained hundreds of small 'minsters' with pastoral as well as devotional functions, serving what may be called the first English parochial system.

The 'old minsters', as they came eventually to be called, served much larger areas than later parish churches. Most of the sources are late, and show them as near-obsolete establishments with only residual authority. Hence we know little of their pastoral work, except that it existed. It appears that the priests, or deputies in the case of strict monks, travelled about within a defined 'parish' preaching to local communities. The 'parishioners' of the minster owed it a render of grain called 'church-scot', and were eventually also obliged to pay it tithes and burial-fees. So complex a system could not have evolved so quickly without royal patronage: Paulinus and Aidan, for instance, preached from residences of their itinerant kings. Church dues were probably based on existing tax assessments, and some kings may have founded several minsters as an act of policy, as Osuiu of Northumbria seems to have done in 655. Kings had an organized system of local government; so, therefore, did the Church. Though eventually smothered by the thousands of little churches which sprang up within them, minster 'parishes' moulded the whole future development of the Church in the English countryside.

Literacy and Legislation

If kings helped the Church to grow, the Church also enhanced the status of kings. The grandsons of pagan war-leaders were coming to see themselves as God's appointed deputies. With Christianity, too, came literacy: kings could revise and formulate tribal custom to resemble the legislation of the civilized world. Æthelberht of Kent, says Bede, made his laws 'according to the custom of the Romans'. Æthelberht's code, and the later seventh-century codes from Kent and Wessex, suggest a mixture of local tradition with borrowings from the Continent. Whatever their practical usefulness (which is problematic), the kings who made them clearly wanted to seem sophisticated: lawgivers in the classical mould. As the kingdoms were opened more and more to influences from Rome and Gaul, the nature of kingship changed. It was becoming important for rulers to uphold justice and direct the internal affairs of their kingdoms, not merely to win battles. Even the seventh-century codes, with their long lists of fines and penalties, suggest an impressive range of royal authority.

Monastic Towns

Also with the first English churches, we start to glimpse the first English towns. If it is doubtful how often sixth-century rulers had permanent headquarters in the Roman towns and forts, it is certain that seventh- and eighth-century kings and bishops favoured them as sites for cathedrals and minsters. Canterbury, York, Winchester, and Worcester cathedrals were all built within Roman defences, and in 635 the first bishop of Wessex was given the Roman fort at Dorchester-on-Thames, called by Bede a *civitas*, to found his see. Churches and monastic complexes built over abandoned ruins were not in themselves towns. Nonetheless, the most highly organized communities of the age were the cathedrals and minsters; craftsmen, tradesmen, servants, and beggars all gravitated to their doors. Archaeological research is increasingly showing us that the first hints of reawakening urban life are associated with major churches, both in Roman towns and on the more numerous sites with no pre-English origins. A late ninth-century translation of Bede's term *urbana loca* is not, as we would expect, 'towns', but 'minsterplaces'. Scores of English towns began as minsters with lay settlements converging on their gates.

Chapter 4
The Mercian Supremacy

England in the early eighth century was a more sophisticated place than it had been in the early seventh. A united English kingdom was still far away, but the English were now starting to become aware of themselves as an ethnic and cultural unity. Bede may have felt this more keenly than anyone: it is easy to forget how significant is the very title of his greatest work, *The Ecclesiastical History of the English People*. It was because he saw the common destiny of his race fulfilled in the united English Church that he could think of an 'English people'. But are there any signs that secular government was also becoming more comprehensive? This is a hard question to answer, not least because there are more sources. On the one hand, institutions and concepts which show the strong side of eighth-century kingship may not be new, but merely recorded for the first time. On the other hand, the dynastic turmoils which show its weak side may not be new either: it is likely that Bede and his contemporaries glossed over such matters. This at least can be said: the eighth-century Mercian kings wielded as much military power as earlier over-kings; and they lived in a world of greater literacy and legality, of more firmly entrenched rights, which made their power more stable and more capable of development.

Æthelbald and Offa

Æthelbald of Mercia (716–57) inherited much of the influence won by Wulfhere. Written charters recording royal grants were now appearing

5. Silver penny of King Offa. As well as providing a better currency, Offa's coins were of a higher artistic quality than any which had circulated in England since the Romans left.

in some quantity, so we can see how kings liked to style themselves. Æthelbald's titles are impressive, if self-conferred. 'King not only of the Mercians but of all the provinces called by the general name Southern English', as one charter calls him, echoes Bede's statement that the early over-kings 'held sway over all the provinces south of the River Humber'. The claim can be supported to the extent that charters show him influencing Kentish affairs and controlling London. But Wessex remained independent, as did Northumbria under Bede's patron King Ceolwulf: Mercian supremacy was never to go north of the Humber.

Æthelbald's successor Offa (757–96) was the most powerful English king before Alfred. His position once secured (which took some years), his conduct in all the kingdoms except Northumbria and Wessex seems to have been more that of a direct ruler than a remote overlord. Earlier kings had suppressed small royal dynasties, but Offa suppressed great ones. For substantial periods he exercised effective power in Kent, and after an unsuccessful coup against Offa's successor in 798, the ancient Kentish dynasty was extinguished for ever. The last king of Sussex appears as one of Offa's *duces*; in Surrey, which had been West Saxon territory, we find Offa confirming a grant by a Mercian noble. In East Anglia (though here the dynasty reappeared later), the *Chronicle* notes laconically for 794: 'In this year Offa, king of Mercia, ordered [King] Æthelberht's head to be struck off.' In Wessex, royal power and tradition were stronger: the kingdom only recognized Mercian protection between 786 and 802, and even then the lordship seems to have been of a much vaguer kind than in Kent.

Offa's standing is emphasized by a famous letter to him from the great Frankish king, Charlemagne. Charlemagne addresses him as an equal, 'his dearest brother', and speaks of 'the various episcopal sees of your kingdom and Æthelred's' as though Offa of Mercia and Æthelred of Northumbria were the only kings in England. The Frankish connection is important (though possibly too much has been made of this one document: there had always been plenty of contact between Gaul and the southern English). Offa would certainly have liked to be thought another Charlemagne, and whatever the reality of royal power, its prestige rose in line with developments abroad. In 787 Offa had his son Egfrith made joint king of the Mercians by a solemn consecration which Northumbria copied nine years later. The semi-sacred character of kingship was becoming stronger.

This did not make dynasties more stable. Succession was uncertain: long after Offa, kings would still be 'chosen' from the royal stock. Any vaguely eligible candidate with forces behind him could aim at the throne, and Mercia, Wessex, and Northumbria were all torn by dynastic feuds during the eighth century. In his efforts to secure the succession, Offa seems to have been as ruthless towards relatives as he was towards neighbours. When his son Egfrith died shortly after Offa himself, the Northumbrian scholar Alcuin saw it as a judgement: 'The vengeance for the blood shed by the father has now reached the son; for you know very well how much blood his father shed to secure the kingdom on his son.'

If much of this shows Offa in a savage light, we must remember that the surviving sources for his reign are mainly external and unsympathetic. His cultural achievements may have been greater than the surviving fragments suggest, and from the 770s we can start to see fundamental innovations in government, local organization, and the exercise of royal power. These were inspired partly by the Frankish example, partly by the now rich and well-established English Church. Offa has some claim to be considered a Church reformer: in 786 he held the only Church council in the Anglo-Saxon period to be attended by papal legates, and if his attempt – successful in the short term – to raise the see of Lichfield into an archbishopric was politically driven, it could also be interpreted as a sensible and much-needed piece of reorganization. Æthelbald and Offa were often involved in Church councils and sometimes presided over them; their thegns and ministers witnessed the decisions, which were recorded in writing. The way Church business was conducted can hardly have failed to heighten the sense of precedent and legality. Though the context is ecclesiastical, such assemblies must have helped to transform the *ad hoc* band of warriors around a seventh-century king into a government and administration which were more organized, and which eventually can even be called bureaucratic.

Fortifications

The duty of landowners to help in the building of bridges and fortifications first appears in a document of 749, and is usually stipulated in later grants of land. This is significant in an age which produced massive public works of at least two kinds: one long-famous, the other only recently understood. The first is, of course, Offa's Dyke, so called by an ancient and probably correct tradition. Recent excavations suggest that this enormous earthwork was a continuous barrier between England and Wales, running from sea to sea. Offa is known to have raided into Wales, but the Dyke is best seen as a defensive rather than an offensive work, built to stop Welsh attacks and cattle-raids across the border. But the fact that it exists at all is proof of the huge resources which Offa commanded.

The charter references to 'fortress-work' imply fortified strongholds rather than dykes. Later, Alfred of Wessex and his heirs would develop a network of large communal fortresses or *burhs* to protect Wessex against the Vikings. More recently, though, archaeology has started to show that some Mercian centres, such as Hereford and Winchcombe, were surrounded by eighth-century banks and ditches, and even had elements of planned street systems. Especially important is Tamworth, where the court stayed regularly from the 790s and which emerges as the nearest thing to a 'capital' in pre-Viking England: excavations have found not only a defended circuit, but also a massively constructed ninth-century mill. Apparently for the first time, Anglo-Saxon rulers (like their earlier British counterparts) were deploying resources to build and maintain fortified citadels; with organized supply systems, the court which had hitherto itinerated between food-collection points could become more sedentary.

Trade and Emporia

We have seen two factors in the emergence of towns: churches and fortresses. The third is obviously trade, both foreign and internal, which seems to have developed rapidly from the 670s. The clearest sign of this is the extraordinary proliferation of small, crude silver coins known as *sceattas*, which by the 720s seem to have been circulating in eastern and southern England in their millions: the first mass currency in Britain since Roman times. In the second half of the century more formal pennies were produced under Frankish influence, first in East Anglia but most notably in the form of Offa's beautiful portrait coins. While it is still unlikely that all transactions were in money, its widespread circulation must have greatly facilitated trade, as well as making it easier for rulers to tax commercial profits.

A dispute between Charlemagne and Offa in 789 reveals that English merchants were habitually using Frankish ports: England and Francia were part of a growing world of international commerce. For nearly a century, in fact, trading centres had been developing throughout northern Europe. This was the age of the *-wics*, a remarkable series of international emporia which appeared around 700 on the coasts of north-west Europe and of southern and eastern England. Each of the major English kingdoms seems to have had its *-wic*: Southampton (*Hamwic*) for Wessex, Ipswich for East Anglia, York (*Eoforwic*) for Northumbria, perhaps Sandwich for Kent. It now seems likely that the biggest of them all was London (*Lundenwic*), called by Bede 'an emporium of many peoples coming by land and sea', which lay not in the walled city but westwards around the Strand and Covent Garden. Excavation on all these sites has revealed intensive settlement and craft production. If primarily they were entrepôts for foreign traders, it is becoming increasingly apparent that they developed commercial hinterlands extending far inland. While our sources do not allow any precise measure of economic growth, it is clear that the internal as well as the overseas economy of England was being transformed in the age of Æthelbald and Offa.

The Church

The eighth and early ninth centuries were a rather unsettled time for the English Church. Lay foundation and patronage brought its own problems, as aristocrats eager to enjoy the tenurial and tax advantages of 'bookland' (land held by written charter, hithero a purely ecclesiastical form of tenure) built monasteries on their estates. Some of these, complained an outraged Bede, were little more than 'fronts' for tax evasion, and while it may be wrong to take this literally there can be little doubt that as the monastic culture proliferated through lay society, there was a decline from the highest late seventh-century standards. Bede was not alone in worrying: a series of reforming synods, notably the great council of *Clofesho* in 747, complained that drunkenness and secular songs were prevalent in monasteries and that monks lived like nobles. Relations between Church and State were not always easy, especially with a king like Æthelbald who seems to have combined monastic reform with robbing minsters and seducing nuns. Dealings between the king and the archbishop of Canterbury tended to be complicated by the strong anti-Mercian feeling in Kent. Archbishop Jaenberht was outraged when Offa raised Lichfield to an archiepiscopal see, and the scheme was abandoned after the king's death on the grounds that it had been prompted by enmity towards the people of Kent.

On the positive side, the English Church did produce one outstanding scholar, Alcuin. A product of the cathedral school at York, he was a leading figure in Charlemagne's court and took a central part in Charlemagne's great revival of classical learning and education. It is significant, especially in the context of Charlemagne's letter to Offa, that the dominant intellectual of late eighth-century Europe was an Englishman: Alcuin, like Bede before him, was a Northumbrian. The culture of Mercia is almost wholly lost to us: it had no Bede to record its achievements, and its greatest monasteries were sacked by the Vikings. Fragments of decorative art, such as the sculptures in the minster of Breedon on the Hill, suggest sumptuous physical surroundings. A noble monument to the age of Æthelbald and Offa is the great minster church of Brixworth, Northamptonshire. It is a sign of how much we do *not* know that this monastery falls to appear in any early document.

The most impressive fact about the eighth-century Church is that the English were now taking Christianity to their original homelands on the Continent. The mission began, oddly enough, through St Wilfrid's quarrel with Archbishop Theodore. Setting out in 678 to state his case at Rome, Wilfrid travelled through pagan Frisia and spent a year preaching. The Frisians were well known to the English from their merchants, and Wilfrid opened the way to more ambitious missionary work. A group of Northumbrians landed in Frisia in 690. Among them was Willibrord, who took the lead and was consecrated archbishop of Frisia in 695. He established his cathedral at Utrecht, and the organized Church of Frankish Frisia developed quickly. Willibrord's work was supplemented by a West Saxon mission led by St Boniface. Between his arrival in 718 and his murder by pagans in 754, Boniface preached among the Frisians, Germans, and Franks, setting up a see at Mainz. As well as converting pagan areas Boniface had great influence on the Frankish Church as a whole, regulating it and bringing it under papal guidance. Through his career he relied on books, recruits, and advice from England, and there survives a large correspondence with friends at home. Much of the work which transformed the old Frankish Church into the expanding Church of the Carolingian revival was done by English men and women.

Chapter 5
The Viking Invasions and the Rise of the House of Wessex

Mercian power did not long outlast Offa. His successor, King Coenwulf, kept hold of Kent and Sussex and even gained some new territory from the northern Welsh, but Wessex slipped from his grasp in 802. A new dynasty of overlords was about to appear, this time West Saxon. In 825 Ecgberht of Wessex won a decisive victory near Swindon, expelled a Mercian under-king from Kent, and annexed Kent, Essex, Surrey, and Sussex. Four years later, Mercia itself fell to Ecgberht, and even Northumbria acknowledged his lordship. This spectacular reversal, and the sudden rise of Wessex to the position of leading player, need some explanation. Two main factors may be suggested: the growing wealth of the West Saxon monarchy, fuelled by the mineral resources of recently conquered Cornwall; and the capacity of Ecgberht's family to determine inheritance and royal succession by agreement rather than by bloodshed, which obviated one of the crippling weaknesses of earlier English kingship.

Viking Attack

Whether such internal strengths on their own would have brought ultimate supremacy will never be known. Under the year 789 the *Anglo-Saxon Chronicle* contains an ominous entry: the first breath of a storm that was to sweep away all rivals to the house of Wessex, and with them some of the best achievements of English civilization:

In this year Beorhtric [*king of Wessex*] took to wife Eadburh, daughter of King Offa. And in his days came first three ships of Norwegians from Horthaland: and then the reeve rode thither and tried to compel them to go to the royal manor, for he did not know what they were: and then they slew him. These were the first ships of the Danes to come to England.

This Viking landing was a minor affair, though there are other references soon afterwards to 'sea-borne pagans' attacking the south coast. More serious, and incomparably more distressing, were raids in the north, for they involved the successive plundering of Lindisfarne (793), Jarrow (794), and Iona (795). Britain had been safe from foreign attacks for two centuries; the reaction to the sudden desecration of three of its most holy places is easily imagined. These were, however, isolated incidents, and it was a generation before the Viking nuisance became a major threat. But a big raid on Kent in 835 opened three decades in which attacks came almost yearly, and which ended with the arrival of a full-scale invading army.

The Invasion of the 860s

The dramatic expansion of the Norwegians and Danes is a European phenomenon, of which the raids on England and Ireland were only one part. Two races were involved (the word Viking, 'pirate', was coined by their victims and refers equally to both), and several motives. They were far from being total barbarians, and by the 840s they had been heavily involved in trade for some generations. It was, indeed, this trade which opened up regular contact with the nations to the west and south. Population grew, and it became hard to find a reasonable living at home. Many adventurers must have heard stories of the fertile lands with monasteries full of easy plunder, and it is surprising rather than otherwise that the early raids were not followed up more quickly.

These factors help to explain why raiders descended in such numbers on

European countries from the 850s onwards, and why casual plundering gave way to a policy of conquest and settlement. There seem to have been two main routes: one around the north of Scotland to the Western Isles and so southwards, the other to the east and south coasts of England and to Gaul. Hence the raids and settlements in Ireland, Scotland, Wales, and Cornwall were mainly Norwegian, while those in the English and Frankish lands were mainly Danish.

In 865 the Danish 'Great Army', led by Halfdan and Ivarr the Boneless, landed in East Anglia. After a few months' stay it turned northwards into Northumbria, which happened to be split by a dynastic dispute, and captured York in 867. Both the rival kings perished, and the Danes set up their own nominee to rule Northumbria as a client state. The army then advanced into Mercia, but on meeting opposition it withdrew to York without an open fight, and in 869 descended again on East Anglia. The inhabitants were defeated in battle, and their king Edmund (soon to be venerated as St Edmund the Martyr) was killed. Within three years, the once-great kingdoms of Northumbria and East Anglia had ceased to exist.

In 870 the Danish army camped at Reading and prepared to invade Wessex. But here the opposition was better organized. After Ecgberht's death the West Saxons were ruled by his son Æthelwulf, a capable ruler whose good planning meant that his four sons could succeed peacefully in order of age. When the Vikings attacked, the third son, Æthelred, was on the throne; the name of his brother and heir, Alfred, was to become the greatest in Anglo-Saxon history.

It was a combined force under Æthelred and Alfred which met the Danes on the Berkshire Downs and inflicted their first serious defeat. But the English success was short-lived. The Danes withdrew to Reading, but almost immediately advanced again and defeated Æthelred and Alfred near Basingstoke. In April 871 a new Danish army landed. Invasion of Wessex seemed imminent, and its defenders had nowhere to turn for help. In the midst of this crisis Æthelred died, and his brother became king of the West Saxons.

Alfred

Alfred the Great (871–99) is known to everyone as the king who saved England against seemingly hopeless odds. This is not quite how contemporaries would have seen it. In political terms at least, 'England' still did not mean very much. The first writer known to use *Angelcynn* (literally '[the land of] the English folk') was Alfred himself, and *Englaland* does not appear for another century. It was not a foregone conclusion that the other kingdoms would accept West Saxon lordship, or even prefer it to the Danes. They might well have chosen kings of their own, and there was always a danger that English rivals, exiles, or disaffected groups would enlist Viking support. The destruction of the other dynasties did not automatically make Alfred king of all the English; he and his heirs achieved this through a mixture of military success, tactful diplomacy, and good luck.

The reign started badly, and after a year of minor defeats Alfred had to buy the Danes off. They left Wessex alone for five years, during which they invaded Mercia, expelled King Burgred, and replaced him with their own nominee: a third ancient kingdom had gone for good. The Great Army now split into two halves. One, led by Halfdan, turned north and began dividing up Yorkshire for permanent settlement. The other, led by Guthrum, Oscytel, and Anund, turned south, and in 875–6 launched another attack on Wessex. At first their success was limited; in 877 they withdrew again to partition out Mercia, and another group split off to colonize Lincolnshire, Nottinghamshire, Derbyshire, and Leicestershire.

Thus it was a much-reduced force which attacked Wessex for the third time in 878. However, a surprise attack on Chippenham gave them the upper hand; much of Wiltshire and Hampshire submitted, and Alfred was driven back to a refuge at Athelney in the Somerset marshes. The position seemed hopeless, but Alfred bided his time in his fortress and gathered troops. Early in May, says the near-contemporary writer of the *Chronicle*:

> he rode to 'Egbert's Stone' . . . and there came to meet him there all the men of Somerset and Wiltshire and part of Hampshire . . . and they rejoiced to see him. And one day later he went from those camps to Iley Oak, and one day later to Edington; and there he fought against the entire host, and put it to flight.

The victory was sudden but decisive. The Danish leader Guthrum accepted baptism with several of his captains, and the two kings settled peace terms. These recognized the Danish occupation of much of England as a fait accompli. The frontier ran roughly north-westwards from London into the north-west midlands; Guthrum was to withdraw with his troops behind this line, where he was to be recognized as king of an independent kingdom. By the autumn of 880 the Danes had left Wessex and western Mercia, and had begun the systematic settlement of East Anglia.

This was not the end of the conflict. In 886 Alfred captured London, apparently after defeating a Danish garrison. In 893 a big Danish army landed in the Thames estuary and raided through England during the next three years, but this time it made little impression on Wessex. Alfred had been busy, both in securing the safety of his own kingdom and in consolidating his lordship over the other territory west and south of the Danish frontier. For the first task, he seems to have improved both the army and the navy. Kings had long been entitled to levies of troops raised in accordance with the land assessment in hides. Alfred's reorganization, by which only half of the army was to be on service at any one time, foreshadows the later 'select *fyrd*' or militia: it must have produced a smaller but more efficient host. An obvious way of combating sea-borne raiders was with more ships, and Alfred is said to have built vessels much bigger than the Vikings', carrying 60 oars or more.

The most important element in his programme – certainly the one which saved Wessex from further inland raids – built on Mercian precedents such as Tamworth and Hereford. By the late 880s Wessex was covered with a network of public strongholds, several of which have a regular grid of streets and can only be described as planned fortified towns. A document called the *Burghal Hidage* lists 30 of these *burhs*, with three more which may be later additions. Perhaps the most impressive case is Winchester, where a new grid ignoring the Roman streets was laid out within the Roman walls. The same linearity can be seen at Oxford, Chichester, Wareham, and others. Planning was remarkably systematic, and it seems that the surveyors used a standard 66-foot measure for setting out the streets. The larger *burhs* were more than just fortresses, and soon acquired an important role in the local rural economy. The burden of manning and maintaining the defences was imposed through hidage assessments on neighbouring landowners, who could use the defended area for their own purposes.

6. The Alfred Jewel. This object, found near Alfred's refuge at Athelney, is inscribed 'Alfred had me made', and almost certainly belonged to the king. Of gold, rock-crystal, and enamel, it illustrates the wealth of the West Saxon court.

Often they built 'town houses' in the *burh* to store their produce for marketing: Domesday Book records several links between urban tenements and rural manors. Traders and craftsmen followed, and the strongholds of the late ninth century became the thriving towns of the late tenth and eleventh. Defence happened to coincide with the needs of a growing economy; thus Alfred has his unexpected but permanent memorial in the road systems of several modern towns.

Like his predecessors and successors, Alfred had the great advantage of being known as a good lord. Thus the free (i.e. western) Mercians could see self-interest in accepting his rule, and a firm alliance, cemented by the marriage of Alfred's daughter Æthelflaed to the Mercian leader Æthelred, brought what was left of the old kingdom permanently into the West Saxon orbit. The 'Lord and Lady of the Mercians' co-operated with Alfred and his son, especially in joint offensives against the Danes. If Alfred was more truly 'king of the English' than anyone before him, it was not just through military strength or because no rivals remained: people genuinely wanted him because they knew that he and his family were just and considerate rulers.

Damage and Repair

But there remained the problem of the Danes and the damage they had done. Some of it was irreparable: whatever happened now, the world of Bede and Offa had gone for ever. The size of the Danish Great Army may be disputed, but it is impossible to deny the evidence of three kingdoms destroyed, dioceses disrupted, innumerable monasteries plundered, charters and other documents almost completely lost for much of eastern England. The ruin of monasteries was perhaps the most serious, for the great houses had been the main repositories of learning and culture, while the small ones were still mainly responsible for pastoral care in the countryside.

In the Danelaw (as eastern and north-eastern England was later known),

Danish soldiers quickly established a society of their own. Yorkshire, Lincolnshire, Leicestershire, and to a lesser extent East Anglia, are full of place-names ending in *-by*, *-thorp*, and other Scandinavian elements. While this is less likely to reflect cataclysmic disruption, as used to be thought, than progressive social change (the English zones also experienced a renaming as more landlord-based structures developed), it certainly shows how thoroughly the area was now inhabited by Danish-speaking peoples. Even when the Danelaw was Christianized and brought under English rule it retained distinctive traditions of social organization, land measurement, and law. Tenth-century kings had the problem of reconciling the claims of a united kingdom with customs very different from those of the English.

England badly needed a revival of literacy and learning, and to this Alfred devoted his last ten years. Like Charlemagne, he carried out his programme of education through a circle of court intellectuals. In some ways his own contribution to this project is the most remarkable of Alfred's achievements. He was the only English king before Henry VIII who wrote books. Lamenting the destruction of manuscripts and the decay of scholarship, he learnt Latin and translated works into English for his subjects' benefit. Among the many translations which his circle produced (and which include, significantly, Bede's *Ecclesiastical History*), several are now known with near-certainty to be Alfred's own work. It is also believed that the *Anglo-Saxon Chronicle*, as we now have it, may have been first compiled at Alfred's court. For all that he deprecated vernacular literacy as second-best, the most remarkable aspect of Alfred's renaissance was that it was based on the language of ordinary people: it pointed the way to the coming expansion of business, government, law, and literature in written English. Alfred was lucky that future events caused so many of his various schemes to bear fruit. Even allowing for this, he remains the outstanding figure of early English history.

The Royal House of England

The reigns of Edward the Elder (899–924), Athelstan (924–39), and Edmund (939–46) were dominated by the reconquest of the Danelaw. This half-century was the formative period for national kingship. Dynastic feuds were avoided, partly through Alfred's careful provision for the succession and partly through some lucky chances. In 902 a dangerous split was averted when Edward's cousin, who had sought Danish help to win the crown, was killed in battle. Athelstan succeeded smoothly in 924 because he was both the rightful heir to Wessex and had been educated in his Mercian aunt's household. By the mid-century there was no serious possibility that Mercia, still less any other kingdom, could revert to an older dynasty. The royal house of Wessex was the royal house of England.

The campaigns of Edward's reign were mainly directed by the king himself in partnership with his sister Æthelflaed of Mercia. The English offensive began when a Danish raid into Mercia was defeated in 910. Over the next eight years, Edward pushed into the Danelaw while his sister kept the Danes busy on their Mercian frontier. Æthelflaed was now threatened from two directions, for Norwegian Vikings from Ireland had begun attacking the west coast. Her main achievement was to build a series of new Mercian *burhs*: on the east frontier against the Danes, on the west frontier against the Welsh, and in the north-west to block Norwegian raids on Tamworth from the Dee and Mersey. In 917 Æthelflaed took Derby, giving Edward a chance to invade East Anglia while the enemy was occupied. Soon all the southern Danelaw had fallen to Edward, though isolated Danish armies were holding out in Stamford, Leicester, Nottingham, and Lincoln. Leicester submitted to Æthelflaed, but her death soon afterwards forced Edward to halt the campaign while he secured Mercia. Returning swiftly, he took Stamford, Nottingham, and Lincoln, and by the end of 920 the English frontier was fixed at the Humber.

Meanwhile, Edward was forming links with his other non-English neighbours. In 918 he received the 'submissions' of the Welsh kings of Gwynedd and Dyfed. In 923, says the *Chronicle*, 'the king of Scots and the whole Scottish nation accepted him as father and lord: so also did Raegnald and the sons of Eadwulf and all the inhabitants of Northumbria, both English and Danish, Norwegians and others; together with the king of the Strathclyde Welsh and all his subjects'. These were the first in a series of such 'submissions', culminating in an extraordinary spectacle in 973 when eight 'British kings' swore fealty to Edward's grandson Eadgar and rowed him on the River Dee.

It must be emphasized that these were personal submissions to the kings to whom they were made: they involved the acceptance of lordship and protection, not the permanent surrender of independence. In fact, Scotland and Wales were both advancing towards their own internal unity. In *c.*850 Kenneth Mac Alpin, king of the Scots, had annexed the Pictish kingdom, and over the next two centuries Scotland developed under Scottish (as against Pictish) rule. In Wales, politics were transformed by the sudden expansion of Gwynedd from the late ninth century onwards, leaving only Dyfed of the smaller kingdoms. The Anglo-Saxons never conquered Wales or Scotland, and in each a native power had emerged dominant by 1066. Nonetheless, Wales was much influenced both by England and by the Vikings.

Among the many groups competing for land in tenth-century Britain was a new one – the Norwegians from Ireland. They had no fondness for the Danes, and their main object was to gain control of the northern Danelaw. In 918 a force led by Raegnald attacked Scotland, based itself in Northumbria, and the following year took York, where Raegnald established himself as king. The Norse kingdom was to last, with interruptions, for 35 years, during which trade grew and the twin Norse cities of York and Dublin expanded fast. Excavation at York has revealed streets of timber houses and shops, laid out by the Danes and redeveloped by Raegnald's followers. During the reigns of Athelstan and

Edmund, the enemies of the English were the Norwegians more than the Danes.

In 920 Edmund had accepted Raegnald's fealty and thus acknowledged his status. But when a new Norse king tried to seize his inheritance in 926, Athelstan attacked and captured York, destroyed its defences, and received the submission of the kings of Scotland and Strathclyde. It is from 927 that Athelstan can be regarded as truly 'king of the English'. Six years later, relations between Athelstan and the Scots broke down. Fearing invasion, the various rivals of the English made common cause. But in 937 the English army under Athelstan defeated a combined force of Norse, Scots, and Strathclyde Welsh. Athelstan was now at the height of his power, king of the English and Danes and in some sense overlord of the British. He was respected by foreign powers, and formed marriage alliances with the French and German royal families. His charters show the Welsh princes regularly attending his court; Hywel Dda, king of Dyfed in Athelstan's time, imitated English silver pennies and issued laws modelled on English codes.

But much still depended on the individual king. Soon after Athelstan's death in 939, a Norse army returned under Olaf Guthfrithson. The new king, Edmund, was forced to recognize Olaf as king of York and its dependent territories. Olaf died in 941, and during the next four years Edmund recovered the northern Danelaw and ravaged Strathclyde. In a contemporary poem, Edmund features as liberator of the Danes from their Norse oppressors: the great-grandsons of Alfred's enemies could identify with the English Crown rather than with their fellow Scandinavians. But in 947, the year after Edmund's death, York fell yet again to a Norse king, Eric Bloodaxe. The next six years saw a confused struggle between Eric, the new English king, Eadred, and a Norwegian rival named Olaf Sihtricson. In 954 Eadred invaded Northumbria, this time for good, and the last king of York was driven out and killed.

Map 2. England in the tenth century.

National Kingship and Local Government

From nearly 50 years of complex warfare the house of Wessex had emerged triumphant. The stable reign of Eadgar (959–75) proves that more had been created than mere military power. Eadgar was not a conqueror: one historian has written that 'his part in history was to maintain the peace established in England by earlier kings'. But this was no mean achievement: the kingdom was young, and it is with Eadgar that the main developments in late Saxon kingship come into focus.

From Athelstan onwards, kings made laws more frequently and went into more detail. They cover a wide range of subjects – peace-keeping, the suppression of thieves, the hierarchy of churches, the conduct of merchants and markets, to name only a few. There is an emphasis on unity: Eadgar's codes make allowance for local custom, especially in the Danelaw, but insist that 'the secular law shall stand in each folk as can best be established'. Building (in this as in much else) on Carolingian models, these kings fostered a concept of public peace, which it was the king's function to enforce, and the duty of all subjects to maintain. Regular assemblies of a larger and more formal royal council (*witenagemot*, literally 'meeting of wise men') are recorded in charter witness-lists. Although in no sense a representative assembly or 'parliament', this was a forum for solemn public acts such as the choosing of kings and issuing of laws. Royal authority was spread wider, and went deeper, than in any other tenth-century European country of comparable size.

The king's will operated through a much-improved system of local government. During the tenth century, the regional anomalies of England were progressively reduced to a single framework of 'shires'. Some had existed for a century or more, and many were based on still older boundaries. But it was essentially under Eadgar and his successors that the English counties stabilized in the form which lasted until 1974, a thousand years later. The shires were entrusted to a group of leading magnates, the ealdormen. In ninth-century Wessex there had been an ealdorman for each shire, but by a gradual process, which seems to start under Athelstan, the number of ealdormen fell and their status rose. By Eadgar's reign the ealdorman was becoming less like a local official, and more like his successor the eleventh-century earl. But he still remained in regular touch with the government of the shires under his care.

For legal and administrative purposes the shires were broken down into subdivisions, called 'hundreds' in most counties, and 'wapentakes' in the northern Danelaw. Each hundred had its own court for settling local business, and communal obligations to provide troops and oarsmen came to be assessed by the hundred. Even this was not the bottom of the ladder: for law enforcement the population was organized into groups of ten mutually responsible households or 'tithings'. The weight of royal government reached the individual peasant through a structure of remarkable complexity. How much was new in the tenth century is hard to say. The principle of the hundred appears in earlier law-codes, and it seems likely that late Saxon hundreds were often or usually based on older territories. But the system was rationalized and improved by Alfred's successors, and under Eadgar it emerges clearly in its developed form.

Another mark of royal strength was the coinage. Even before Alfred, the kings of Wessex and Mercia and the archbishop of Canterbury had agreed on a standard currency of silver pennies. Decrees issued by Athelstan between 924 and 939 order that 'one coinage shall run throughout the land'. He and his heirs maintained a remarkable consistency in size and weight, and all coins were minted by strictly controlled moneyers in boroughs and other local centres. In c.973 Eadgar designed a new coinage of pennies, which was regularly renewed and remained the basis of the English currency until long after the Conquest. The excellence of the coins shows a degree of control which was, once again, unique in contemporary Europe.

The Monastic Reform

A personal achievement of Eadgar was to encourage monastic reform. True Benedictine monasticism seems to have been almost dead in early tenth-century England. Several great and innumerable small minsters had been destroyed by the Danes, while those which survived had tended towards a more secular lifestyle. Groups of minster priests lived in separate houses with their wives and children; in their everyday existence they came closer to cathedral canons than to monks. A successful reconstruction of English monasticism would need models to emulate, and money. The first was provided by the great European reform movement, of which the English reform was essentially a part; the second was provided by Eadgar and his nobility. Three aristocratic churchmen, St Dunstan, St Æthelwold, and St Oswold, were the main agents for introducing Continental ideas to English houses.

The West Saxon kings had shown an interest in strict monasticism – though only as one among several acceptable forms of the religious life – since Alfred, and it was through royal patronage that two houses were reformed in the 940s: Glastonbury by Dunstan and Abingdon by Æthelwold. What was unusual about Eadgar was his willingness to embrace wholeheartedly the exclusive, 'all-monastic' stance of the reformers, especially the extreme and belligerent Æthelwold. From the 960s, with Dunstan, Æthelwold, and Oswold installed in the sees of Canterbury, Winchester, and Worcester, a solid platform existed for a court-driven reform: by the end of the century, nearly 50 houses had been refounded under the influence of Glastonbury, Abingdon, and Oswold's monastery at Westbury-on-Trym.

The monks in the reformed monasteries followed a way of life based on the rule of St Benedict, with elaborations in ritual and daily routine in line with Continental practice; the main influences were from Ghent in the Low Countries and Fleury on the Loire, where Dunstan and Oswold respectively had studied. In c.970 the various traditions were combined

7. King Eadgar portrayed on the foundation charter of New Minster, Winchester, dated 966. This picture, one of the finest examples of the Winchester School of manuscript illumination, illustrates the close connection between royal authority and the great monastic reform movement.

in the *Regularis Concordia*, one rule for all the English houses to follow. Mainly because England had the strongest European monarchy, the king's role as promoter of the movement and patron of the reformed houses was more prominent than in the Continental reform. Nonetheless, great aristocrats put considerable resources into the movement: to found a monastery was once again a socially prestigious act.

The new houses were wealthy, respected, and endowed with treasures and fine buildings. Literary sources hint at the richness of English art under Eadgar. A number of the magnificent illuminated books survive, but only fragments of the gold, enamel, and ivory ornaments, and almost none of the major buildings. Fate has been unkind to late Anglo-Saxon architecture, for all the greatest churches were rebuilt after the Conquest. As enlarged in the tenth century, the minster at Winchester was 250 feet long, with side-chapels, elaborate western towers, and carved and painted friezes. But it must be stressed that this spiritual and material regeneration touched only a fraction (probably under 10 per cent) of the old communities: the others continued as before. Thus at the Norman Conquest the Benedictine houses co-existed with an unknown number – probably some hundreds – of small secular minsters, relics of the pre-Viking Church.

If the new monasticism owed much to Europe, it was distinctively English in its relations with the state and society at large. By 1000 most English bishops were monks, and both bishops and abbots deliberated with lay magnates in the king's council. Great churchmen were among the most valued advisers of the last Anglo-Saxon kings. Equally, Church reform added lustre to a king who set much store by the sacred character of his office. Eadgar's coronation in 973 was postponed until he reached 30, the minimum canonical age for ordination to the priesthood. The climax of the ceremony was not the crowning, but the anointing with holy oil which conferred near-priestly status and set the king above human judgement. As the homilist Ælfric of Eynsham put it, 'no man can make himself king, but the people have the free will to choose him to be king who is most pleasing to them. But once he has been consecrated king he has power over the people, and they may not shake his yoke from their necks.' The frontispiece of the Winchester New Minster foundation charter shows Eadgar as he wanted to be seen: crowned, standing between two saints, and offering his gift to the heavenly king through whom earthly kings rule.

Chapter 6
Æthelred and Cnut: The Decline of the English Monarchy

The next two reigns would show that there were still great limitations to West Saxon kingship of England. On Eadgar's death in 975, court factions grouped around his two young sons. Edward ('the Martyr') succeeded, but was soon murdered and replaced by his brother Æthelred. This was an appropriate start for an unhappy reign. Æthelred 'the Unready' (978–1016) has always had a bad press (though his famous nickname has lost its original meaning, which involved the pun *Æthelræd Unræd*, 'Noble-Counsel No-Counsel'). Probably he did lack the qualities which were still so important for kingship: the knack of putting trust in the right places and commanding trust in others. On the other hand, law and justice continued to develop in his reign under the guidance of the learned Archbishop Wulfstan. If it had not been for a new problem – the return of the Vikings – the English state might have held together as well as it had done under Eadgar.

Æthelred

The new raiders were even more dangerous than their ninth-century ancestors. By the 970s the Danish king, Harold Bluetooth, who had gained control of both Denmark and Norway, was creating a formidable army of highly trained professional soldiers. In 988 Harold was deposed by his son Swein, who maintained his father's army and built large fortresses to house military communities. One of these has been excavated at Trelleborg in Denmark. It consists of a large circular earthwork enclosing groups of great boat-shaped halls, all planned with mathematical precision. Both Trelleborg and the Danish sagas suggest a degree of co-ordination and discipline which the English army would have found it hard to match.

The attacks began within a year or two of Æthelred's accession. At first they were on a fairly small scale, but in 991 a large Danish force defeated Alderman Byrhtnoth and the Essex militia at Maldon, and had to be bought off with a large payment. The pattern was repeated after heavy raids in 994, 997, and 1002. It is for these payments that Æthelred's reign is now so notorious. Huge numbers of his pennies have been found in Scandinavia, and several Swedish tombstones commemorate mercenaries who went to England and enriched themselves with tribute. In the 990s, as in 1066, England's wealth was also its danger.

How was Æthelred to cope? One measure was to prevent the harbouring of Vikings by his neighbours, and for geographical reasons the young duchy of Normandy was the most important of these. The Normans were only a few generations away from their own Viking ancestors, and had sometimes opened their ports to raiders returning from England. But in 991 King Æthelred and Duke Richard made a treaty against aiding each other's enemies, and ten years later Æthelred married the duke's daughter. So began the fateful association of Normandy and England.

Hitherto the king's internal policy does not seem to have been very different from that of his predecessors. He inherited a powerful, well-established aristocracy, and his early charters show him building up support with grants of land just as Eadwig and Eadgar had done. But from 1002 the Viking threat became rapidly more severe, and exposed a basic weakness in royal power. The king's lands, and probably his activities generally, were still heavily concentrated in Wessex. The resources with which he could buy support in the north and east were very limited – and these were just the areas where support most needed to be bought. They still had separatist tendencies, and contained many people who remembered their Danish origins. Æthelred's later charters show a shift of patronage into the Midlands and eastern England, and new men of non-Wessex origin become prominent. The king was struggling to hold England united and in a state of defence. His ineptitudes may have made the task harder, but nobody would have found it easy.

The strain on the government was demonstrated when, in 1002, Æthelred and his council ordered a massacre of all the Danes living in England. This extraordinary command cannot have been fully enforced – in some areas the population was largely Danish – but it hints at something approaching national hysteria. We know that, when the Danes in Oxford took refuge in St Frideswide's minster church, the citizens burnt it down. This massacre almost certainly prompted the Danish invasion of the following year, led by King Swein himself. Swein sacked Norwich, but his East Anglian campaign involved heavy losses and in 1005 he withdrew to Denmark. Next year he returned, led his army through Berkshire, Wiltshire, and Hampshire, and once again had to be bought off with a large payment. In the ensuing respite the government built a new fleet, but early in 1008, 80 of the ships were burnt through the treason of an English captain. On the heels of this misfortune, another Danish army landed, led by Thorkill the Tall and Hemming. In 1009 they burnt Oxford, and then moved to East Anglia, from where they raided into Kent the following year. The campaign ended unexpectedly in 1012 when Thorkill changed sides, disgusted by his own army's brutal murder of Archbishop Ælfheah. This brought 45 ships into Æthelred's service; the rest of the army left England.

The feebleness of England's defences was now clear to all, and when Swein returned in 1013 it was with the intention of conquest.

Disillusioned with Æthelred's government, the men of the Danelaw welcomed a Danish king and accepted Swein almost immediately. By the end of the year he had taken Oxford, Winchester, and London, and Æthelred had fled to exile in Normandy. In February 1014 Swein died; his son Harold succeeded to his Scandinavian empire, but the army in England accepted Harold's younger brother Cnut as their king. Meanwhile Æthelred had returned, and by spring he was fielding an expedition against the Danes. Caught unprepared, Cnut withdrew to Denmark. In 1015 he was back with a bigger force, to find that Æthelred's son Edmund Ironside had taken control of the northern Danelaw in defiance of his father. During the next few months Cnut recovered Northumbria and then moved towards London. But before the Danish forces arrived Æthelred was dead and Edmund had been proclaimed king. Even in Wessex, however, many men accepted Cnut's lordship without a struggle. Edmund rallied his forces, and for a little while it seemed that the Danes might still be driven back. But in the autumn of 1016 Cnut won a decisive battle at Ashingdon in Essex. The treaty which followed left Edmund with only Wessex, and when he died shortly afterwards Cnut became king of all England.

Cnut

King Cnut (1016–35) had to deal with problems which were not dissimilar to those which faced King William 50 years later. Like William, Cnut set out to rule not as a conqueror but as a rightful English king. He married Æthelred's widow, and acted ruthlessly to secure the throne: several leading English magnates were killed. Once secure, Cnut adopted with enthusiasm the traditional attributes of civilized kingship. He issued laws and founded monasteries; in the words of a chronicler of the next century, he changed himself 'from a wild man into a most Christian king'. Yet he was still a Dane, and on his brother's death in 1019 he inherited a great northern empire of which England was only part. During the 1020s he became more and more involved in Danish affairs.

The breadth of Cnut's involvements is the main reason for his changes in England, which were relatively few, but in the end damaging.

Naturally he had many followers eager for rewards. There was no full-scale replacement of the English landowning class such as occurred after 1066, but a good many Danes joined the aristocracy. An alien and therefore rather insecure king, Cnut kept a regiment of household troops or 'housecarls' who were a considerable burden on the country. After 30 years of paying to keep the Danes away, landowners now had to pay to support a Danish standing army. The destruction of the well-integrated aristocracy of tenth-century England was soon to put severe strains on the country's unity.

Cnut also had to make English government function during his long absences abroad. In 1017 he divided the kingdom into four earldoms – Northumbria, East Anglia, Mercia, and Wessex. This ran obvious risks of reviving local separatist feeling, especially since the Northumbrian and East Anglian earls were both Danes. By the end of the reign the most important figures were Siward earl of Northumbria, Leofric earl of Mercia (whose wife was Lady Godiva of Coventry fame), and Godwine earl of Wessex. Godwine's origins are obscure, but by the 1030s he and his family were the wealthiest and most powerful laymen below the king. Cnut's earldoms are largely responsible for the power politics which dominate the last 30 years of Anglo-Saxon history.

Chapter 7
The End of the Anglo-Saxon Kingdom

When Cnut died in 1035 there were several possible successors. The Wessex dynasty was represented by Æthelred's younger sons Edward and Alfred, now at the Norman court, and by Edmund Ironside's son, who was exiled in Hungary. Cnut had two sons by two wives: Harold, by Ælfgyfu of Northampton, and Harthacnut, by Emma the widow of Æthelred. Cnut had wanted Harthacnut to succeed to his whole empire. But while Harthacnut delayed in Denmark the council appointed Harold as regent (despite the opposition of both Emma and Godwine), and in 1037 made him king. The previous year, the English prince Alfred had unwisely visited England and died of injuries inflicted at Godwine's instigation. Harthacnut was recalled after Harold's death in 1040, but when he died two years later the Danish royal line ended. Almost everyone now wanted to restore the ancient dynasty of Wessex. Æthelred's son Edward had been living for a year at the English court, and in 1042 he was elected king.

Edward 'the Confessor' (1042–66) was destined to be venerated as the principal English royal saint. His modern biographer, scrutinizing the reality behind the pious legend, writes that 'he was not a man of great distinction. But neither was he a holy imbecile. He was, like many of his rank and time, a mediocrity.' Whatever his strengths and weaknesses, he inherited the strongest government in eleventh-century Europe. The reason for this strength lay partly in institutions which were centuries old, partly in the very disruptions of the last 60 years.

The Institutions of Government

Local government had developed since Eadgar's day. On the one hand, the great earldoms consolidated under Cnut had given huge territorial power to a few men. An insecure king now had to face the threat of over-mighty subjects. On the other hand, an invaluable new official had appeared to carry out royal policy in the localities. During Æthelred's reign one of the king's local bailiffs ('reeves') in each shire had come to be known as the 'shire-reeve' or sheriff. He was the king's chief executive agent in the shire, and gradually assumed more and more of the alderman's functions. The sheriff was responsible for collecting royal revenues and the profits of justice, but he also belonged to the growing community of local thegns. In the shire court he could announce the king's will to the gentry of the shire, take a big part in day-to-day business, and add the weight of royal authority to action against oppressive magnates. The shire court and the sheriff are among the most important Anglo-Saxon legacies to later medieval government.

A highly efficient tax system had evolved as a direct result of England's weakness under Æthelred. The huge sums paid to the Danes in the 990s had to be raised from the country. The 'geld', as it came to be called, was based on the ancient method of assessing land in hides, and was raised at a fixed rate of so much per hide. Between 1012 and 1051 it was levied yearly by the successive kings, though now for maintaining their standing armies. The complex system of assessment developed for this purpose is the basis of the later Domesday Book, and it is an extraordinary tribute to the early eleventh-century English bureaucracy that the Norman kings continued to raise Danegeld for nearly a century after the Conquest.

This period also saw a new type of official document: the royal writ. Writs were possibly issued by Æthelred and certainly by Cnut, but the earliest which now survive as originals are from Edward's reign. In its

8. A sealed writ of Edward the Confessor, in favour of Westminster Abbey.

initial form, the writ was a brief notification to the shire-earl and the sheriff or bishop that a grant of land had been made and should be witnessed in the shire court. A typical example reads:

> Edward the king greets Harold the earl and Tofi his sheriff and all his thegns in Somerset in friendly fashion. And I make known that Alfred has sold to Giso the bishop the land of Lutton peacefully and quietly: he did this in my presence at Parret, and in the presence of Edith my wife, Harold the earl and many others who were there present with us. We also wish that the same bishop shall hold that land with all its appurtenances which the bishop possesses with sac and soc [jurisdictional rights over land] as freely as any of his predecessors as bishops ever did anything. And if anything be taken away from it unjustly we ask that it may be restored. Nor shall it be done otherwise.

This combined efficiency with a new means of authentication: a pendent wax seal, stamped from a die kept in the king's household. As title-deeds, writs provided useful supplements to the old formal charters, which were unwieldy and easily forged. They also provided a means for the king to make his will known quickly and clearly in the shires. William the Conqueror soon adapted the writ for issuing orders, and all the more important types of post-Conquest royal document are descended from it.

When ordering a taxation or issuing a writ, the king would have consulted his secretariat. Edward the Confessor, like kings since Alfred at the latest, had a clerical staff of priests, headed by a chief clerk whose office developed into that of the medieval chancellor. One of their duties was to keep records: from the late Anglo-Saxon period comes evidence of very detailed surveys recording land-tenure, numbers of hides, and tax obligations. Some remarks by Bede suggest that even the seventh-century Northumbrian kings had enough precise information to grant land in exact numbers of hides, and embedded in a text known to us as the Tribal Hidage may be seventh-century assessment memoranda relating to peoples and provinces dependent on Mercia. So we can be confident that ninth- and tenth-century kings had fiscal records of some kind, though how detailed is impossible to say. By Edward the Confessor's reign, the royal secretariat possessed rolls which listed the hidages of shires and hundreds, the amount of royal land they contained, and perhaps even the names, owners, and values of individual manors. We know this not from the documents themselves (though a few fragments survive), but from Domesday Book. The great survey of 1086 could scarcely have been compiled so quickly and so thoroughly if the commissioners had not had access to earlier lists. The loss of the pre-Conquest public records is tragic, but the mere knowledge that they existed says much for the quality of Edward's administration.

Changes in Society

If English government changed greatly between the reigns of Alfred and Edward, so too did English society. The mid-ninth to mid-eleventh centuries saw rapid growth in the population and economy. Before Domesday Book there are no statistics, but written, archaeological, and topographical evidence gives some strong hints that many aspects of later English society crystallized in these years. Not surprisingly, more people meant bigger towns. By the Conquest there were English towns in a sense that we would understand today: large concentrations of people with markets and traders, groups of craftsmen in specialized quarters, guilds and regulations, numerous churches, and in some cases rapidly expanding suburbs. The late Anglo-Saxon law codes recognize trading centres or 'ports' (not necessarily coastal) and large boroughs, rated according to the number of moneyers they were allowed to contain. The towns included most of the Alfredian *burhs* and many minster centres, but they were not confined to places of ancient importance. We cannot even guess at the number of local markets, but a good many which first appear in the thirteenth century may be older than they seem.

9. A late Anglo-Saxon drawing of a wheeled plough, pulled by a team of oxen.

The emergent towns were part of a rapidly developing countryside. Topographical studies suggest a process of settlement nucleation in the more populous areas, with the inhabitants of scattered farms clustering into villages. At the same time, agriculture was becoming more complex and more integrated, so that by 1066 many parts of England had 'common fields', farmed by peasants with intermingled holdings, and therefore probably with corporately agreed cropping patterns. The early development of field systems is controversial, but it is in the tenth century that we can first detect the basic contrast between the open-field zone of Midland England and the surrounding 'wood-pasture' areas. Much remains uncertain about the relationship between changes in settlement form, agriculture, and land-holding, but it seems that the process went through several stages and continued well beyond the Conquest. There are also suggestions that sometimes these were not spontaneous developments, but rearrangements planned from above. Peasant society was becoming more stratified and cohesive, and lords were making greater demands on their tenants.

One reason is that there were more manors and more manorial lords. Except in retarded areas, most of the old 'multiple estates' had fragmented by the eleventh century into units corresponding in size to modern rural parishes. Population grew, cultivation expanded, and the components of the old 'extensive' systems became self-contained entities. Many more charters survive from the tenth century than from the eighth and ninth together; most of them grant smaller units of land, and the proportion in favour of the laity is higher. The aristocracy were settling down: although they still defined themselves in military terms, they begin to seem less like warriors, more like country gentry. Archaeology shows that by 1000 the countryside was becoming dotted with manor-houses, sometimes defended. The class of small thegns had broadened into a rural squirearchy, and Domesday Book shows that in 1066 England contained hundreds of manorial lords.

This is the context in which most parish churches were founded. Just as kings and bishops had built minsters in the seventh and eighth centuries, so thegns built manorial churches in the tenth and eleventh. The minster parishes were slowly decaying, and more and more of the manors within them were acquiring rival churches of their own, served by manorial priests. This crucial stage in the development of pastoral organization was evolutionary and informal, essentially a matter of private enterprise. Eleventh-century churches (both before and after the Conquest) were in effect 'owned' by their lords, and their functions were determined on tenurial rather than pastoral lines: the church's function was to serve the needs of the lord, his household, and tenants. We can scarcely speak of anything so formal as a 'parochial system', though the raw materials were there: probably more than half the parish churches existing in 1700 were founded before 1066.

So the familiar landmarks of rural England – villages, manor-houses, churches – took shape mainly in the late Anglo-Saxon period. For Archbishop Wulfstan, writing around 1000, the last two were normal marks of thegnhood: 'If a *ceorl* prospered so that he possessed fully five hides of land of his own, a church and a kitchen, a bell and a fortress-gate, a seat and special office in the king's hall, he was worthy thereafter to be called a *thegn*.' The 'fortress-gate' in this famous passage leads to a question which has become needlessly controversial: were there castles in pre-Conquest England? One writer, equating private castles with feudalism and convinced that late Saxon England was non-feudal, argues that it contained no fortresses beyond the communal *burhs*. But if a strongly fortified manor-house counts as a castle, the existence of castles says little about a society except that it included a land-based aristocracy of some status. In fact excavation now proves that fortified houses did exist, and complex manorial buildings surrounded by banks and ditches of *c.*1000–50 have been found at Sulgrave, Northamptonshire, and Goltho, Lincolnshire. These sites show that ordinary late Saxon thegns' residences could be as imposing as most manor-houses of the twelfth and early thirteenth centuries.

Warfare was becoming more professional, and equipment consequently more expensive. By the end of the tenth century, a system of military service had developed in which every unit of five hides was responsible for providing and equipping one man for the *fyrd* (militia). This acknowledged that the average farmer could not reasonably be expected to kit himself out from his own resources, and by implication raised the status of the fighting man. Five hides, according to Wulfstan, were a *thegn*'s minimum estate, and armour and weapons had become another mark of *thegn*hood. The fully armed late Saxon warrior was something more than a *ceorl* turned soldier.

By Æthelred's reign the monastic reform was running out of steam. Burton Abbey in Staffordshire (1004) and Eynsham Abbey in Oxfordshire (1005) were the last great foundations, and the general political disruption and draining of resources soon put a stop to large-scale patronage and building. Edward's piety did, however, produce one building project, the most ambitious that England had ever seen. In about 1050 he began to rebuild the old minster church at Westminster on a scale worthy of the English monarchy. Architecture in England was stagnant, but in Normandy its development during the last 40 years had been spectacular: the finest buildings of Eadgar's day would have looked unimpressive beside the abbey churches of Bernay and Caen. So for Westminster Abbey Edward looked to Norman architects, though his church as eventually built was magnificent and innovative even by their standards, and probably owed something to English decorative traditions. It is somewhat ironic that the last great monument of the house of Wessex was mainly a product of Norman culture.

The Problem of the Succession

The final years of Anglo-Saxon history are dominated by Godwine's family and the problem of the succession. Edward had married Godwine's daughter, but by the early 1050s it had become clear that he would never produce an heir. Edward, son of Edmund Ironside, returned

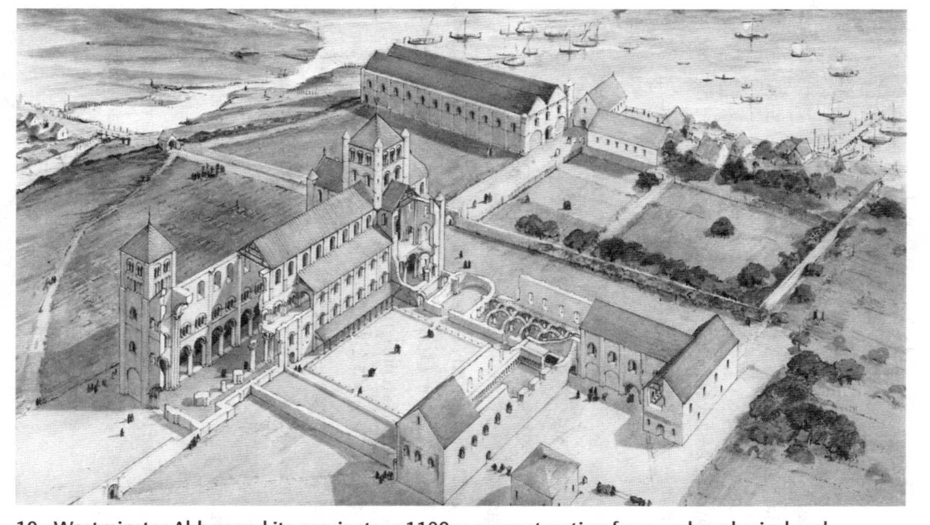

10. Westminster Abbey and its precincts, *c.*1100: a reconstruction from archaeological and documentary evidence and surviving buildings (after Gem and Ball, 1980). In the foreground is the Abbey church, built by Edward the Confessor and destroyed in the thirteenth and fourteenth centuries. Westminster Hall, in the background, was rebuilt by William II.

from Hungary with his infant son in 1057 but died almost immediately. The young prince Eadgar was the legitimate heir, but nobody can have viewed with much enthusiasm the prospect of a child on the throne. The Norwegian king, Magnus, and after him his son Harold Hardrada, saw themselves as the heirs to Cnut's empire, including England. Neither candidate is likely to have appealed much to King Edward: his eyes, if they were turned anywhere, were turned across the Channel. The duchy of Normandy, where he had lived in exile for 25 years, had developed fast in strength and internal organization. In 1035 Duke Robert had been succeeded by his bastard son William, then a boy of seven. We will never know for certain if Edward promised his throne to William, but the story is not inherently unlikely.

Edward had never forgiven Godwine for his brother's murder, and the tension between them came to a head in 1051. One of Edward's Norman friends became involved in a brawl at Dover, and several men were killed. Edward ordered Godwine, as earl of Wessex, to sack Dover in retribution. Godwine refused and raised troops against the king, who summoned the Mercian and Northumbrian earls with their full forces. Conflict was avoided; as a contemporary put it, 'some of them considered it would be great folly if they joined battle, because wellnigh all the noblest in England were present in those two companies, and they were convinced they would be leaving the country open to the invasion of our enemies'. Godwine's support crumbled, and he and his family went into exile. Over the next year Edward increased the Norman element at court, but in 1052 Godwine returned with a large fleet and the king was obliged to be more compliant. The Norman archbishop fled home, and several of his fellow countrymen were banished at Godwine's request.

Godwine now enjoyed virtually supreme power, but in 1053 he died. His successor in the earldom of Wessex was his son Harold, destined to be the last Anglo-Saxon king. When Earl Siward of Northumbria died two years later, his earldom went to Harold's brother Tostig. Thanks to the activities of King Gruffydd of Gwynedd, the standing of Godwine's sons soon rose yet higher. Gruffydd, who had recently made himself supreme in Wales, allied with the exiled heir to the Mercian earldom and launched a series of attacks into English territory, in the course of which Hereford was sacked and burnt. The combined forces of Harold and Tostig drove Gruffydd back into Wales, and in 1063 caused his downfall and death. With this success behind him, Harold was the outstanding figure in England. Despite his lack of royal ancestry, he seemed an obvious candidate for the throne.

But in 1064, or perhaps early in 1065, Harold visited Duke William in Normandy. He went, say the Norman sources, as Edward's ambassador, to swear an oath confirming an earlier promise of the English Crown. It is possible, but on the whole unlikely, that the story of the oath is a Norman invention. But there is a third explanation, the one which the English artists of the Bayeux Tapestry may secretly be trying to give us: Harold falls into William's hands by mischance, is forced to swear the oath, and returns shamefacedly to a horrified King Edward. Whichever version is true, many contemporaries believed that William had right on his side as well as might.

The Norman Conquest and After

The events of the last two years moved quickly. During 1065 Northumbria rebelled against Earl Tostig. Harold mediated, but the local nominee was upheld: Tostig went into exile, henceforth his brother's enemy. On 5 January 1066 King Edward died. Urgent military need over-rode legality, and the council elected Harold as king. This was the signal for his two adult rivals. Harold Hardrada of Norway was the first to move: aided by the exiled Tostig, he invaded Northumbria during the summer and occupied York. Harold, who was awaiting the expected invasion from Normandy, was forced to move north. At Stamford Bridge near York he met and defeated the Norwegian forces on 25 September.

Hardrada and Tostig were both killed, and King Harold recovered Northumbria.

Meanwhile Duke William's fleet, which had been delayed by bad weather, landed at Pevensey on 28 September. Harold rushed southwards; but the preparations which he had made two months earlier had fallen apart, and the core of his army was exhausted. On 14 October 1066, the English and Norman armies met near Hastings. Harold's forces gathered on the crest of a hill and formed a wall of shields. The battle lasted all day, and at first the English position seemed strong. Apparently it was lost through lack of discipline rather than lack of force. Sections of Harold's army seem to have been enticed down the slope in pursuit of real or feigned retreats, and then cut off and overwhelmed. Gradually the English troops were broken up; the centre held until dusk, but the outcome was already clear when Harold fell on the spot marked in later centuries by the high altar of Battle Abbey.

William advanced to Dover and then to Canterbury, where he received the submission of Winchester. But his main objective was London, for there the core of the English resistance had gathered under Eadgar Atheling. Meeting opposition at London Bridge, William encircled the city leaving a trail of devastation. Meanwhile the Atheling's party was crumbling, and when William reached Berkhamsted the English nobles, headed by Eadgar himself, met him and offered their fealty.

Alfred's dynasty, which had survived Danes, Norsemen, and Danes again, had succumbed at last to foreign invasion. It was the end of the road for the house of Wessex, but not for Anglo-Saxon society, or for its institutions and culture. It was essentially by English means that the Norman kings ruled England, and after the traumatic interlude of conquest the structures which had made the state so strong between Eadgar and Edward the Confessor reasserted themselves. In a variety of ways, England in 1400 looks startlingly like England in 1000. Hundreds survived into modern times; shires and sheriffs are still with us; the

English language is still spoken. Most fundamentally, it was in the years between 600 and 1100 that English towns, villages and the road-system, and much of the distinctive character of the countryside, took shape.

Further Reading

Original Sources *

Gildas: The Ruin of Britain and Other Documents, ed. and trans. M. Winterbottom (Chichester, 1978), the only contemporary source for the Anglo-Saxon settlements.

The Gododdin of Aneirin, ed. J. T. Koch (Cardiff, 1997), a late Welsh text, but embodying sources for sixth- and seventh-century north Britain.

Adomnan of Iona: Life of St Columba, trans. R. Sharpe (Harmondsworth, 1995).

Bede: Ecclesiastical History of the English People, trans. J. McClure and R. Collins (Oxford, 1994), a brilliant and vivid narrative written in the 730s; the most important single source for earlier Anglo-Saxon history.

The Age of Bede, trans. J. F. Webb (revised edn, Harmondsworth, 1983), other sources for seventh- and eighth-century England and its religious culture.

The Anglo-Saxon Chronicle, trans. G. N. Garmonsway (London, 1953), the late Anglo-Saxon vernacular chronicle, providing contemporary comment from Alfred's reign onwards.

Alfred the Great, trans. S. Keynes and M. Lapidge (Harmondsworth, 1983), Asser's *Life of Alfred* and related sources.

* Items arranged chronologically by subject

The Earliest English Poems, trans. M. Alexander (2nd edn, Harmondsworth, 1977), translations of the more important Anglo-Saxon poems.
Beowulf, trans. S. Heaney (London, 1999).

General and Political

R. Abels, *Alfred the Great* (Harlow, 1998).
F. Barlow, *Edward the Confessor* (London, 1970).
J. Campbell (ed.), *The Anglo-Saxons* (Oxford, 1982), an outstanding book, with splendid illustrations; easily the best introduction.
D. P. Kirby, *The Earliest English Kings* (London, 1991).
M. Lapidge, J. Blair, S. Keynes, and D. Scragg, *The Blackwell Encyclopaedia of Anglo-Saxon England* (Oxford, 1999), the most comprehensive reference aid.
H. R. Loyn, *The Governance of Anglo-Saxon England, 500–1087* (London, 1984).
P. Stafford, *Unification and Conquest: A Political and Social History of England in the Tenth and Eleventh Centuries* (London and New York, 1989).
F. M. Stenton, *Anglo-Saxon England* (3rd edn, Oxford, 1971), long the standard history, and still of great value.
B. Yorke, *Kings and Kingdoms of Early Anglo-Saxon England* (London, 1990).

The Church

F. Barlow, *The English Church 1000–1066* (2nd edn, London and New York, 1979).
J. Blair and R. Sharpe (eds), *Pastoral Care before the Parish* (Leicester, 1992), local parochial organization and relations between Church and laity.
P. Hunter Blair, *The World of Bede* (London, 1970), religion and learning in eighth-century Northumbria.
H. Mayr-Harting, *The Coming of Christianity to Anglo-Saxon England* (London, 1972), still the best general account of the conversions.

R. Morris, *Churches in the Landscape* (London, 1989), the archaeology and topography of the early Church.

Society, Economy, and Landscape

S. Crawford, *Childhood in Anglo-Saxon England* (Stroud, 1999).

R. Faith, *The English Peasantry and the Growth of Lordship* (Leicester, 1997).

C. Fell, *Women in Anglo-Saxon England* (London, 1984).

M. Gelling, *Signposts to the Past* (London, 1978).

J. Haslam (ed.), *Anglo-Saxon Towns in Southern England* (Chichester, 1984).

D. Hill, *An Atlas of Anglo-Saxon England* (Oxford, 1981).

D. Hinton, *Archaeology, Economy and Society: England from the Fifth to the Fifteenth Century* (London, 1990).

D. Hooke, *The Landscape of Anglo-Saxon England* (London, 1998).

G. Owen-Crocker, *Dress in Anglo-Saxon England* (Manchester, 1986).

Scotland and Wales

B. E. Crawford, *Scandinavian Scotland* (Leicester, 1987).

W. Davies, *Wales in the Early Middle Ages* (Leicester, 1982).

A. A. M. Duncan, *Scotland: The Making of the Kingdom* (Edinburgh, 1975).

K. Hughes, *Celtic Britain in the Early Middle Ages* (Woodbridge, 1980).

A. P. Smyth, *Warlords and Holy Men: Scotland, AD 80–1100* (London, 1984).

Archaeology and Art

J. Backhouse, D. H. Turner, and L. Webster (eds), *The Golden Age of Anglo-Saxon Art, 966–1066* (London, 1984).

R. Bailey, *England's Earliest Sculptors* (Toronto, 1996).

M. Carver, *Sutton Hoo: Burial Ground of Kings?* (London, 1998).

E. Fernie, *The Architecture of the Anglo-Saxons* (London, 1983).

G. Henderson, *From Durrow to Kells: The Insular Gospel-Books 650–800* (London, 1987).

L. Webster and J. Backhouse (eds), *The Making of England: Anglo-Saxon Art and Culture AD 600–900* (London, 1991).

M. Welch, *Anglo-Saxon England* (London, 1992).

D. M. Wilson (ed.), *The Archaeology of Anglo-Saxon England* (Cambridge, 1976), chapters by several authors on the various kinds of physical evidence.

D. M. Wilson, *Anglo-Saxon Art* (London, 1984).

S. Youngs (ed.), *'The Work of Angels': Masterpieces of Celtic Metalwork, 6th–9th Centuries AD* (London, 1989).

Chronology

c.450	The *adventus Saxonum*: Hengest and Horsa settle in Kent (traditional date)
455	Hengest rebels against Vortigern (traditional date)
477	Saxon settlement of Sussex (traditional date)
495	Saxon settlement of Wessex (traditional date)
c.500	Battle of *Mons Badonicus* (traditional date)
577	West Saxons capture Gloucester, Cirencester, and Bath (traditional date)
597	St Augustine's mission arrives in Kent
616	Raedwald of East Anglia, as over-king, makes Eadwine king of Northumbria
c.624	Death of Raedwald, and his probable burial in the Sutton Hoo barrow
627	Conversion of Eadwine and the Northumbrian court
633	Battle of Heavenfield; Oswald of Northumbria becomes over-king
635	Conversion of King Cynegils of Wessex
642	Oswald is killed at Oswestry by King Penda of Mercia
655	Penda is defeated and killed at the *Winwaed* by Osuiu of Northumbria, who becomes over-king
664	Synod of Whitby
669	Arrival of Archbishop Theodore
672	Synod of Hertford; battle of the Trent, marking the beginnings of the rise of Mercia

685–8	Expansion of Wessex under Caedwalla to include Kent, Surrey, and Sussex
716	Æthelbald becomes king of Mercia
731	Bede completes his *Ecclesiastical History*
747	Council of Clofesho
757	Death of Æthelbald; Offa becomes king of Mercia
786	Legatine Council held under Offa
793–5	Danish raids on Lindisfarne, Jarrow, and Iona
796	Death of Offa
825	Ecgberht of Wessex defeats Mercia and annexes Kent, Essex, Surrey, and Sussex
835	Big Danish raid on Kent
865	The Danish 'Great Army' lands
867	Northumbria falls to the Danes
869	East Anglia falls to the Danes; murder of St Edmund
871	The Danes attack Wessex; Alfred becomes king
874	Mercia falls to the Danes
878	(March) The Danes drive Alfred into the Somerset marshes (May) Alfred defeats the Danes at Edington; Guthrum is baptized
899	Death of Alfred; Edward 'the Elder' becomes king of Wessex
910–20	Edward and Æthelflaed reconquer most of the Danelaw
919	Norse kingdom of York is founded by Raegnald
924	Death of Edward; Athelstan becomes king
937	Athelstan defeats the Norse, Scots, and Strathclyde Welsh at Brunanburh
939	Death of Athelstan; Edmund becomes king
940	Dunstan begins to refound Glastonbury as a regular monastic house
946	Death of Edmund
954	The last king of York is deposed
959	Eadgar becomes king
960	Dunstan becomes Archbishop of Canterbury
c.970	*Regularis Concordia* is compiled

973	Eadgar is crowned and consecrated, and receives the submission of British princes
975	Death of Eadgar; Edward 'the Martyr' becomes king
978	Murder of Edward; Æthelred 'the Unready' becomes king
991	The Danes defeat Alderman Byrhtnoth and the Essex levies at Maldon; treaty between England and Normandy
1002	Æthelred orders the massacre of all Danes in England
1003	Danish invasion led by King Swein
1013	Swein returns with a new army; the Danelaw accepts him as king
1014	Swein dies; the Danish army in England elect Cnut as their king
1016	(April) Æthelred dies; Edmund 'Ironside' becomes king (Autumn) Cnut defeats Edmund at Ashingdon; Edmund dies and Cnut becomes king of all England
1017	Cnut divides England into four earldoms
1035	Death of Cnut
1037	Harold becomes king
1040	Death of Harold; Harthacnut becomes king
1042	Death of Harthacnut; Edward 'the Confessor' becomes king
1051–2	Conflict between King Edward and Godwine earl of Wessex
1053	Death of Godwine; his son Harold becomes earl of Wessex
1064–5	Earl Harold visits Duke William in Normandy
1066	(January) Death of King Edward; Earl Harold becomes king (September) King Harold of England defeats and kills King Harold of Norway at Stamford Bridge
1066	(October) Duke William of Normandy defeats and kills King Harold of England at Hastings (December) William is consecrated king

Index

Page numbers in *italics* refer to illustrations or captions. There may also be textual references on the same page.

A

B

F

G

H

Expand your collection of

VERY SHORT INTRODUCTIONS

1. Classics
2. Music
3. Buddhism
4. Literary Theory
5. Hinduism
6. Psychology
7. Islam
8. Politics
9. Theology
10. Archaeology
11. Judaism
12. Sociology
13. The Koran
14. The Bible
15. Social and Cultural Anthropology
16. History
17. Roman Britain
18. The Anglo-Saxon Age
19. Medieval Britain
20. The Tudors
21. Stuart Britain
22. Eighteenth-Century Britain
23. Nineteenth-Century Britain
24. Twentieth-Century Britain
25. Heidegger
26. Ancient Philosophy
27. Socrates
28. Marx
29. Logic
30. Descartes
31. Machiavelli
32. Aristotle
33. Hume
34. Nietzsche
35. Darwin
36. The European Union
37. Gandhi
38. Augustine
39. Intelligence
40. Jung
41. Buddha
42. Paul
43. Continental Philosophy
44. Galileo
45. Freud
46. Wittgenstein
47. Indian Philosophy
48. Rousseau
49. Hegel
50. Kant
51. Cosmology
52. Drugs
53. Russian Literature
54. The French Revolution
55. Philosophy
56. Barthes
57. Animal Rights
58. Kierkegaard
59. Russell
60. Shakespeare
61. Clausewitz
62. Schopenhauer
63. The Russian Revolution
64. Hobbes
65. World Music
66. Mathematics
67. Philosophy of Science
68. Cryptography
69. Quantum Theory
70. Spinoza

71. Choice Theory
72. Architecture
73. Poststructuralism
74. Postmodernism
75. Democracy
76. Empire
77. Fascism
78. Terrorism
79. Plato
80. Ethics
81. Emotion
82. Northern Ireland
83. Art Theory
84. Locke
85. Modern Ireland
86. Globalization
87. Cold War
88. The History of Astronomy
89. Schizophrenia
90. The Earth
91. Engels
92. British Politics
93. Linguistics
94. The Celts
95. Ideology
96. Prehistory
97. Political Philosophy
98. Postcolonialism
99. Atheism
100. Evolution
101. Molecules
102. Art History
103. Presocratic Philosophy
104. The Elements
105. Dada and Surrealism
106. Egyptian Myth
107. Christian Art

VERY SHORT INTRODUCTIONS

Derived from the best-selling *Oxford Illustrated History of Britain*, the following British history titles are now available in the Very Short Introductions series:

- **Roman Britain**
  Peter Salway
- **The Anglo-Saxon Age**
  John Blair
- **Medieval Britain**
  John Gillingham & Ralph A. Griffiths
- **The Tudors**
  John Guy
- **Stuart Britain**
  John Morrill
- **Eighteenth-Century Britain**
  Paul Langford
- **Nineteenth-Century Britain**
  Christopher Harvie & H. C. G. Matthew
- **Twentieth-Century Britain**
  Kenneth Morgan

HISTORY

A Very Short Introduction

John H. Arnold

History: A Very Short Introduction is a stimulating essay about how we understand the past. The book explores various questions provoked by our understanding of history, and examines how these questions have been answered in the past. Using examples of how historians work, the book shares the sense of excitement at discovering not only the past, but also ourselves.

'A stimulating and provocative introduction to one of collective humanity's most important quests – understanding the past and its relation to the present. A vivid mix of telling examples and clear cut analysis.'

David Lowenthal, University College London

'This is an extremely engaging book, lively, enthusiastic and highly readable, which presents some of the fundamental problems of historical writing in a lucid and accessible manner. As an invitation to the study of history it should be difficult to resist.'

Peter Burke, Emmanuel College, Cambridge

www.oup.co.uk/vsi/history

ARCHAEOLOGY

A Very Short Introduction

Paul Bahn

This entertaining Very Short Introduction reflects the enduring popularity of archaeology – a subject which appeals as a pastime, career, and academic discipline, encompasses the whole globe, and surveys 2.5 million years. From deserts to jungles, from deep caves to mountain tops, from pebble tools to satellite photographs, from excavation to abstract theory, archaeology interacts with nearly every other discipline in its attempts to reconstruct the past.

'very lively indeed and remarkably perceptive ... a quite brilliant and level-headed look at the curious world of archaeology'

Barry Cunliffe, University of Oxford

'It is often said that well-written books are rare in archaeology, but this is a model of good writing for a general audience. The book is full of jokes, but its serious message – that archaeology can be a rich and fascinating subject – it gets across with more panache than any other book I know.'

Simon Denison, editor of *British Archaeology*

www.oup.co.uk/vsi/archaeology